Collins

INTERNATIONAL
PRIMARY
ENGLISH

Teacher's Guide 1

I0892148

William Collins' dream of knowledge for all began with the publication of his first book in 1819. A self-educated mill worker, he not only enriched millions of lives, but also founded a flourishing publishing house. Today, staying true to this spirit, Collins books are packed with inspiration, innovation and practical expertise. They place you at the centre of a world of possibility and give you exactly what you need to explore it.

Collins. Freedom to teach.

Published by Collins
An imprint of HarperCollins*Publishers*
The News Building
1 London Bridge Street
London SE1 9GF

1st Floor, Watermarque Building, Ringsend Road, Dublin 4, Ireland

Browse the complete Collins catalogue at www.collins.co.uk

10 9 8 7 6 5 4 3 2 1

ISBN 978-0-00-836775-6

British Library Cataloguing-in-Publication Data
A catalogue record for this publication is available from the British Library.

Author: Joyce Vallar
Series editor: Daphne Paizee
Publisher: Elaine Higgleton
Product developer: Natasha Paul
Project manager: Karen Williams
Development editor: Sonya Newland
Copyeditor: Karen Williams
Proofreader: Catherine Dakin
Cover designer: Gordon MacGilp
Cover illustrator: Petr Horácek
Internal designer and typesetter: Ken Vail Graphic Design Ltd.
Text permissions researcher: Rachel Thorne
Image permissions researcher: Alison Prior
Illustrators: Ken Vail Graphic Design Ltd., Advocate Art, Beehive Illustration and QBS Learning
Production controller: Lyndsey Rogers
Printed and bound by CPI Group (UK) Ltd, Croydon CR0 4YY

With thanks to the following teachers and schools for reviewing materials in development: Amanda DuPratt, Shreyaa Dutta Gupta, Sharmila Majumdar, Sushmita Ray and Sukanya Singhal, Calcutta International School; Akash Raut, DSB International School, Mumbai; Melissa Brobst, International School of Budapest; Shalini Reddy, Manthan International School; Taman Rama Intercultural School.

Acknowledgements
The publishers gratefully acknowledge the permissions granted to reproduce copyright material in the book. Every effort has been made to contact the holders of copyright material, but if any have been inadvertently overlooked, the Publisher will be pleased to make the necessary arrangements at the first opportunity.

Cover illustration: *The Lonely Penguin* Reprinted by permission of HarperCollins*Publishers* Ltd © 2011 Petr Horácek.
The Big Red Bus Reprinted by permission of HarperCollins*Publishers* Ltd © 2006 Alison Hawes, illustrated by Woody Fox; *Pet Cat, Big Cat* Reprinted by permission of HarperCollins*Publishers* Ltd © 2006 Alison Hawes; *Animal Coats* Reprinted by permission of HarperCollins*Publishers* Ltd © 2011 Clare Llewellyn; *In the Forest* Reprinted by permission of HarperCollins*Publishers* Ltd © 2011 Becca Heddle; *Bot on the Moon* Reprinted by permission of HarperCollins*Publishers* Ltd © 2006 Shoo Rayner; *Funny Fish* Reprinted by permission of HarperCollins*Publishers* Ltd © 2005 Michaela Morgan, illustrated by Jon Stuart; *The Small Bun* Reprinted by permission of HarperCollins*Publishers* Ltd © 2006 Martin Waddell, illustrated by T. S. Spookytooth; *The Lonely Penguin* Reprinted by permission of HarperCollins*Publishers* Ltd © 2011 by Petr Horácek.

We are grateful to the following for permission to reproduce copyright material:
Coolabi Group Ltd for the poem on p.48, 'Lion' from *Rumble in the Jungle* written by Giles Andreae and illustrated by David Wojtowycz, Tiger Tales, 2001, text copyright © Purple Enterprises Limited 2016; Grace Andreacchi for the poem on p.57, 'Mister Moon' from *Little poems for children* copyright © Grace Andreacchi; Joyce Vallar for the poem on p.65 'A Fine Feathered Fish' from *Hector Hedgehog's Big Book of Rhymes*, Collins Fun Phonics, copyright © Joyce Vallar; and Macmillan for the poem on p.66 'The Nut Tree' by Julia Donaldson, from *The Gruffalo's Child Song and Other Songs*, text copyright © Julia Donaldson / Axel Scheffler 2012. First published in 2012 by Macmillan Children's Books, an imprint of Pan Macmillan. Reproduced by permission of Macmillan Publishers International Limited

FSC www.fsc.org
MIX
Paper from responsible sources
FSC™ C007454

This book is produced from independently certified FSC™ paper to ensure responsible forest management.

For more information visit: **www.harpercollins.co.uk/green**

Contents

Digital download with audio tracks available at www.collins.co.uk/internationalresources

Introduction

About *Collins International Primary English*

Collins International Primary English is specifically written to meet fully the requirements of the Cambridge Primary English curriculum framework, and the material has been carefully developed to meet the needs of primary English learners and teachers in a range of international contexts.

The material at each level has been organised into nine units, each based around particular text types. The activities in each unit are introduced and explored in contexts related to the selected texts.

The course materials are supplemented and enhanced by a range of print and electronic resources, including photocopiable (printable) master sheets for support, extension and assessment of classroom-based activities (you can find these on pages 104–143 of this Teacher's Guide, as well as on the digital resource). Reading texts are supported by audio-visual presentations.

Components of the course

For each of Stages 1–6 as detailed in the Cambridge Primary English curriculum framework, we offer:

- a full colour, highly illustrated Student's Book with integral reading texts
- a write-in Workbook linked to the Student's Book
- this comprehensive Teacher's Guide with clear instructions for using the materials
- a downloadable digital package, which includes transcripts of the key texts on slideshows, audio files of readings, and printable PCMs.

Approach

The course is designed with learner-centred learning at its heart. Learners work through a range of contextualised reading, writing, speaking and listening activities with guidance and support from their teacher. Plenty of opportunity is provided for learners to consolidate and apply what they have learned and to relate what they are learning both to other contexts and the environment in which they live.

Much of the learners' work is conducted in pairs or small groups in line with international best practice. The tasks and activities are designed to be engaging for learners and to support teachers in their assessment of learner progress and achievement. Each set of lessons is planned to support clear learning objectives and the activities within each unit provide opportunities for oral and written feedback by the teacher, as well as self- and peer-assessment options.

Throughout the course, there is a wide variety of learning experiences on offer. The materials are organised so that they do not impose a rigid structure, but rather allow for a range of options linked to the learning objectives.

Weekly review

A weekly review section is built into the unit-by-unit teaching support in this Teacher's Guide. This review can be used for on-going assessment, as a tool to inform the next steps in teaching and learning.

Achievement levels are likely to vary from learner to learner. To provide support for differentiation, we have labelled the activities with either a square, circle or triangle.

The square, circle and triangle indicate what learners at varying levels might be expected to have achieved each week.

■ The square indicates what can be expected of almost all learners.

● The circle indicates what might be expected of most learners,

▲ The triangle indicates what level of achievement might be expected from learners who need a challenge.

A selection of follow-up activities is provided after each weekly review.

Introduction

Cambridge Global Perspectives™

Cambridge Global Perspectives is a unique programme that helps learners develop outstanding transferable skills, including critical thinking, research and collaboration. The programme is available for learners aged 5–19, from Cambridge Primary through to Cambridge Advanced. For Cambridge Primary and Lower Secondary learners, the programme is made up of a series of Challenges covering a wide range of topics, using a personal, local and global perspective. The programme is available to Cambridge schools but participation in the programme is voluntary. However, whether or not your school is involved with the programme, the six skills it focuses on are relevant to all students in the modern world. These skills are: research, analysis, evaluation, reflection, collaboration and communication.

More information about the Cambridge Global Perspectives programme can be found on the Cambridge Assessment International Education website:
www.cambridgeinternational.org/programmes-and-qualifications/cambridge-global-perspectives.

Collins supports Cambridge Global Perspectives by including activities, tasks and projects in our Cambridge Primary and Lower Secondary courses which develop and apply these skills. The content of the activities encourages practice and development of the Cambridge Global Perspectives skills to support teachers in integrating and embedding them into students' learning across all school subjects. Please note that the activities are not intended to correlate with the specific topics in the Challenges in the Cambridge Primary Global Perspectives curriculum framework.

Activities in this book that link to the Cambridge Global Perspectives are listed at the back of this book on page 144.

Teacher's Guide

The Teacher's Guide offers detailed guidance for covering each unit. Each unit is designed to cover three teaching weeks. The teacher knows their class and context best, so they should feel free to vary the pace and the amount of work covered each week to suit their circumstances. Each unit has a clear structure, with an introduction, suggestions for introducing the unit, lesson outcomes and a resource list of supporting materials that can be used in the unit.

Student's Book

The Student's Book offers a clear structure and easy-to-follow design to help learners to navigate the course. The following features are found at all levels:

- A range of fiction, non-fiction, poetry, play scripts and transactional texts are provided to use as a starting point for contextualised learning. Learners explore language through speaking and reading and then apply what they have discovered in writing. Notes provide a focus on different genres of texts.
- Clear instruction rubrics are provided for each activity. The rubrics allow learners to develop more and more independent learning as they begin to master and understand instructive text.
- All of the reading texts have audio-visual support available as downloadable files. Teachers can play these to the class and learners can use these themselves if they need to listen to the text again.
- Grammar and language boxes provide teaching text and examples to show the language feature in use. These are coloured so that learners can easily recognise them as they work through the course.
- The notepad feature contains reminders, hints and interesting facts.

Workbook

The Workbook is clearly linked to the Student's Book. The activities here contain structured spaces for learners to record answers. The activities can be used as classroom tasks, for homework, or for assessment purposes. The completed Workbook tasks give the teacher an opportunity to check work and give written feedback. Learners have a consolidated record of their work and parents or guardians can see what kind of activities learners are doing in class.

Digital resources

The digital resources are offered as a downloadable package. You can access these at www.collins.co.uk/internationalresources. These resources can be used to support learning and on-going assessment. The unit guidelines in this Teacher's Guide offer suggestions for when and how to use these resources.

Introduction

All of the reading and listening texts in the course have been recorded and are supplied in the downloadable package as audio recordings. The audio recordings offer a range of voices, pace and expression and they will enhance the classroom experience by introducing variety and making it easier for the teacher to observe learners as they listen to, and follow texts.

We suggest that you use the audio recordings as you introduce each reading text. Learners can either listen only or follow the transcript provided on the slides or in their books as they listen to the text. Following and listening allows them to hear the words and the correct pronunciation and also to get a sense of where to pause, where to change expression and how to pace themselves when they are reading aloud.

Some materials can be printed out for use in the classroom. For example, there is an additional activity provided for each unit, with a supporting PCM. These tasks are teacher marked.

E-books

E-books are available for all components. The e-books can be used in a reader view on computer screens and are also designed to be used with interactive whiteboards and if available, iPads and tablets.

Each e-book has standard functionality such as scrolling, zooming, an interactive Contents page and the ability to make notes and highlight sections digitally.

Assessment in Primary English

In the *Collins International Primary English* course, assessment is a continuous, planned process that involves collecting information about learner progress and learning in order to provide constructive feedback to both learners and parents or guardians and also to guide planning and the next teaching steps.

The Cambridge Primary English curriculum framework makes it clear what learners are expected to learn and achieve at each level. Our task as teachers is to assess whether or not learners have achieved the stated goals using clearly-focused, varied, reliable and flexible methods of assessment.

In the *Collins International Primary English* course, assessment is continuous and in-built. It applies the principles of international best practice and ensures that assessment:

- is ongoing and regular
- supports individual achievement and allows for learners to reflect on their learning and set targets for themselves
- provides feedback and encouragement to the learners
- allows for integration of assessment into the activities and classroom teaching by combining different assessment methods, including observations, questioning, self-assessment and informal tasks
- uses strategies that cater for a variety of learner needs in the classroom (language, physical, emotional and cultural), and acknowledges that learners do not all need to be assessed at the same time, or in the same way
- allows for, and prepares learners for, more formal assessment including controlled activities and tasks. Learners should not be tested at all at Stages 1 and 2, and up to Stage 5, formative assessment is preferable to summative.

The *Collins International Primary English* course offers opportunities for consolidation and reinforcement in the form of task sheets that teachers can use to assess learners' knowledge and understanding. These task sheets assess the skills and competencies developed in a cumulative manner. In some cases, learners will use the same texts as context; in other cases, they will be expected to read and make sense of an unseen text and to answer a range of contextualised questions based on that.

At Stage 1, there is a short consolidation task at the end of each unit.

Registered Cambridge International Schools benefit from high-quality programmes, assessments and a wide range of support so that teachers can effectively deliver Cambridge Primary.

The information in this section is based on the Cambridge Primary English curriculum framework from 2020. You should always refer to the appropriate curriculum framework document for the year of your students' tests to confirm the details and for more information. Visit www.cambridgeinternational.org/primary to find out more.

Introduction

Laying the foundations of learning to read in the early stages

To learn to read and write, learners need to be phonologically aware and have a functional understanding of the alphabet, along with an understanding of the purpose and value of print. Successful reading and writing depends on their ability to make the association between all three of these skills.

Learning to read should be treated as an enjoyable problem-solving activity. Learners must be encouraged to use a wide range of strategies to help them to read unknown words.

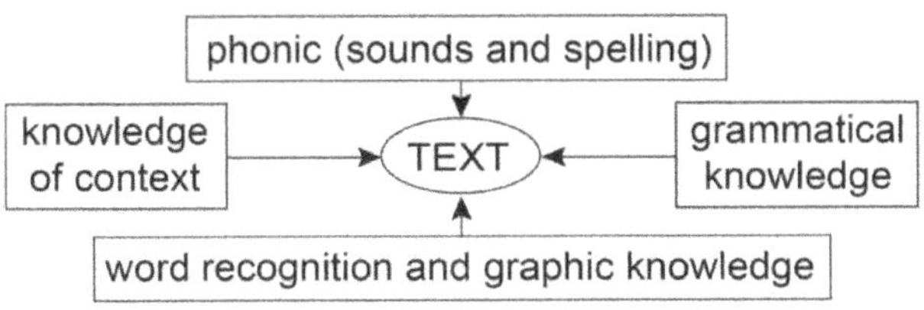

The *Collins International Primary English* Course provides a range of activities which allow learners to apply the phonics and spelling skills they have acquired in the systematic phonics and spelling programmes followed at your school. There are activities in the Student's Book and in the Workbook to cover all the phonics and spelling objectives in the curriculum framework.

First 100 high frequency words

the	and	a	to	said
that	with	all	we	can
are	up	had	my	her
what	there	out	this	have
went	be	like	some	so
in	he	I	of	it
was	you	they	on	she
is	for	at	his	but
find	more	I'll	round	tree
magic	shouted	us	other	food
fox	through	way	been	stop
must	red	door	right	sea
these	began	boy	animals	never
next	first	work	lots	need
that's	baby	fish	gave	mouse
something	bed	may	still	found
live	say	soon	night	narrator
small	car	couldn't	three	head
king	town	I've	around	every
garden	fast	only	many	laughed

Phonics

Phonics is a strategy for teaching reading and spelling of the English language. It focuses on developing the learners' ability to hear, identify and manipulate phonemes, in order to teach the correspondence between these sounds and the spelling patterns that represent them. A phonics programme should foster a steady development of phonological and phonemic awareness.

Phonological awareness is an explicit awareness of the sounds in words, demonstrated by the ability to identify onset, generate rhyme and segment syllables in words.

The smallest unit of sound in a word is called a phoneme. There are approximately 44 phonemes in the English language. A phoneme can be formed by one, two, three or four letters. For example:

c as in 'cot' – one letter

ch as in 'chat' – two letters

–igh as in 'high' – three letters

–tion as in 'station' – four letters

'Cat' has three phonemes (*c-a-t*), but 'chat' also has three phonemes (*ch-a-t*).

The 44 sounds are represented by the 26 letters (graphemes) of the alphabet.

There are a number of skills that should be taught and practised in a phonic programme.

1 Letter sounds (phonemes)

Learning the letter sounds should include alphabet sounds as well as two letters making one sound, like *sh*, *ch*, *ng*. It should also include learning that the same sound can be represented in more than one way, such as *ai*/*ay* representing the long vowel *a* and the same spelling can represent more than one sound, such as *ow* in 'now' and 'show'.

2 Letter formation

Learners should learn to form the letters correctly and consistently.

3 Blending

Learners should learn to blend sounds together to read a word. In order to read an unfamiliar word phonemically, a learner must attribute a phoneme (sound) to each letter or letter combination in the word and then merge the phonemes together to pronounce the word.

Introduction

4 Segmenting

Learners should learn to listen and break a word down into its component sounds, for example *c-a-t*, *sh-o-p*. Learners need to be able to do this to produce a written word (spelling) from a spoken word.

5 Onset and rime

Onset is the initial consonant or consonant cluster of letters (adjacent consonants) in words which precedes the vowel, for example '*b*ag', '*cl*ock'.

Rime refers to the vowel and final consonant(s). For example *–at* in 'cat', *–ing* in 'string' or the final digraph, e.g. *–ow* in 'how', 'now', 'cow'.

When a learner is learning to read and write, there are two crucial things to learn:

- the sounds represented by written letters
- how to blend the sounds together to make a word, and how to break a word into its component sounds (segments) to spell a word.

Alphabet sounds – Learners should be given opportunities to learn the relationship between letter (grapheme) and sound (phoneme) and to hear, read and write the alphabet sounds. At first the focus is on the sound that an alphabet letter represents but learners should learn the names of each alphabet letter and the sound each represents. You should use the words 'name' and 'sound' correctly when speaking to the learners. It is very important when teaching learners the alphabet sounds to remember not to add an *uh* to the end of consonant sounds – so say *mmm* and not *muh*. It is then easier to blend the sounds together to make words. The focus in the beginning is on letters as initial sounds as in '*h*at' and '*p*at', but very quickly every opportunity must be taken to make learners aware that sounds appear at the end of words as in 'ha*t*' and 'ha*d*', and in the middle of words as in 'h*a*t' and 'h*o*t'.

When learners have been taught a group of sounds, they can then learn to blend the sounds to read words made up from those sounds. They can then be taught more sounds and learn to blend those too.

The order in which the sounds are taught will vary depending on which scheme is used in your school, but it shouldn't be alphabetical order as that is not the best order to allow learners to start blending the sounds for reading.

Some sounds are represented by more than one letter, such as *sh* in '*sh*ip', *ch* in '*ch*at'.

The powerful reason for looking at alphabet letters as sounds is to give learners a tool to read words and they must be encouraged to do so at all times. It is important for learners to know the sounds. It is more important for them to use the sounds as a reading strategy.

Concept of rhyme – Learners should also be given the opportunity to develop the concept of rhyme. They should have plenty of opportunities to become familiar with rhymes through listening to, joining in with and reciting and performing rhymes. When learners experience singing, chanting and learning rhymes, they gradually develop a script for building rhyming skills through imitation and experimenting.

The three elements of rhyme are:

- an awareness of rhyme
- the ability to recognise and identify rhyme
- the ability to generate rhyme.

Segmenting and blending – Learners should be given every opportunity to develop an appreciation of blending individual sounds to make words, e.g. *c-a-t*/'cat', *sh-o-p*/'shop' and *b-oa-t*/'boat', and segmenting words into sounds, e.g. 'cat'/*c-a-t*, 'shop'/*sh-o-p* and 'boat'/*b-oa-t*.

They should be given opportunities to build words with letters using their sense of analogy and to see the resemblance between certain words. They should be given opportunities to read new words by changing the initial sound (onset) and by using the rime from the original word. For example:

hat	best	hop	boat
bat	nest	top	coat
fat	pest	shop	moat
sat	rest	chop	float

At the early stages, every day should include some phonic activity. This may be in the form of direct teaching, reading lists of regular words, writing regular words (or using magnetic letters to form words), phonic games and activities, and recapping/highlighting a phonic skill that arises from a text. You should take every opportunity to reinforce the learners' learning by asking about/commenting on phonic skills recently taught.

Introduction

Learning objectives matching grid

The types of reading texts and the objectives covered in each unit are listed here by strand for easy reference.

These learning objectives are reproduced from the Cambridge Primary English curriculum framework from 2020. This Cambridge International copyright material is reproduced under licence and remains the intellectual property of Cambridge Assessment International Education.

<table>
<tr><th colspan="2">1 Going places</th></tr>
<tr><td colspan="2">Texts:
The Big Red Bus (simple recount with familiar settings)
Let's Go Shopping (non-fiction text)
Simple map of bus route (labels and captions)
Dan, Dan (simple rhyme)</td></tr>
<tr><td>Reading</td><td>1Rw.01 Know the name of each letter in the English alphabet and the most common sound (phoneme) associated with it.
1Rw.05 Use phonic knowledge to read decodable words.
1Rw.06 Use phonic knowledge to sound out some elements of unfamiliar words.
1Rv.01 Begin to show understanding of words and sentences encountered in reading.
1Rv.02 Use pictures in texts as cues to support understanding of unfamiliar words.
1Rv.04 Recite the alphabet in order.
1Rv.05 Explore sounds and words in texts, e.g. rhyming words, rhythm.
1Rg.02 Explore in texts, and understand, the use of full stops and different uses of capital letters.
1Rs.01 Talk about the sequence of events or actions in a text, e.g. what happens at the beginning, in the middle and at the end of a story.
1Rs.02 Explore and recognise the features of text structure in a range of different fiction and non-fiction texts, including simple poems. [Stages 1 and 2]
1Rs.03 Explore and recognise parts of a book, including cover, title and contents.
1Rs.04 Explore and recognise how texts for different purposes look different, e.g. different uses of pictures.
1Ri.01 Read and explore a range of simple stories and poems, including identifying the contribution of any visual elements. [Stages 1 and 2]
1Ri.05 Explore explicit meaning in simple texts. [Stages 1 and 2]
1Ri.06 Retell a familiar story verbally, including most of the relevant information.
1Ri.08 Find information by reading labels, lists and captions.
1Ri.11 Make simple inferences based on events in a text.
1Ri.12 Respond verbally to simple questions about texts read or heard.
1Ri.13 Answer questions about texts with some explanation of thinking. [Stages 1 and 2]
1Ra.01 Enjoy reading and hearing a range of simple stories, poems and non-fiction texts. [Stages 1 and 2]
1Ra.03 Read aloud simple texts independently.
1Ra.04 Talk about texts heard or read, including making links with own experiences and expressing likes and dislikes.</td></tr>
<tr><td>Writing</td><td>1Ww.01 Identify the most common letter(s) (grapheme(s)) associated with each sound in the English language.
1Ww.05 Choose plausible graphemes that match phonemes to write simple regular words and to attempt other words.
1Ww.06 Spell familiar words accurately, including common exception words.
1Wv.01 Use vocabulary relevant to a familiar topic. [Stages 1 and 2]
1Ws.01 Develop a simple sequence of known actions or events, e.g. by ordering sentences and then adding to them.
1Wp.04 Record answers to simple questions about texts, e.g. in lists.
1Wp.05 Present text in a range of different ways, e.g. diagrams with typed labels, storyboards with handwritten captions. [Stages 1 and 2]</td></tr>
<tr><td>Speaking and Listening</td><td>1SLm.01 Speak audibly and clearly with familiar people.
1SLm.02 Provide relevant information, as needed.
1SLs.01 Listen and respond appropriately, including following a sequence of simple instructions.
1SLs.02 Ask simple questions about what is heard or read.
1SLg.01 Work with others in a group. [Stages 1 and 2]
1SLg.02 Show understanding of the opinions of others. [Stages 1 and 2]</td></tr>
</table>

	1SLg.03 During a discussion, listen to others without interrupting. **1SLg.04** Take turns in speaking, expressing own feelings and ideas. **1SLp.04** Engage in imaginative play, enacting simple characters or situations. **1SLr.01** Talk about own activities, including what they enjoyed.

2 Having fun	
Texts: *Rev and Dev* (simple story with a familiar setting, written in rhyme)	
Reading	**1Rw.01** Know the name of each letter in the English alphabet and the most common sound (phoneme) associated with it. **1Rw.02** Identify the sounds (phonemes) represented by more than one letter (consonant digraphs; vowel digraphs; trigraphs, e.g. 'th', 'sh', 'ch', 'ai', 'ee', 'igh'). **1Rw.04** Read verbs with endings *–s*, *–ed*, *–ing*. **1Rw.05** Use phonic knowledge to read decodable words. **1Rw.06** Use phonic knowledge to sound out some elements of unfamiliar words. **1Rw.07** Begin to recognise a range of common words on sight, including common exception words. **1Rv.01** Begin to show understanding of words and sentences encountered in reading. **1Rv.02** Use pictures in texts as cues to support understanding of unfamiliar words. **1Rv.04** Recite the alphabet in order. **1Rv.05** Explore sounds and words in texts, e.g. rhyming words, rhythm. **1Rg.02** Explore in texts, and understand, the use of full stops and different uses of capital letters. **1Rg.04** Explore in texts sentences that contain *and*. **1Rg.06** Explore in texts examples of nouns and verbs. **1Rs.02** Explore and recognise the features of text structure in a range of different fiction and non-fiction texts, including simple poems. [Stages 1 and 2] **1Rs.03** Explore and recognise parts of a book, including cover, title and contents. **1Ri.01** Read and explore a range of simple stories and poems, including identifying the contribution of any visual elements. [Stages 1 and 2] **1Ri.02** Identify the characteristics of simple stories. [Stages 1 and 2] **1Ri.05** Explore explicit meaning in simple texts. [Stages 1 and 2] **1Ri.07** Identify the main characters in a story and talk about what happens to them. **1Ri.12** Respond verbally to simple questions about texts read or heard. **1Ri.14** Show understanding of rhyme and repetition when joining in with reading familiar simple stories and poems. **1Ra.01** Enjoy reading and hearing a range of simple stories, poems and non-fiction texts. [Stages 1 and 2] **1Ra.02** Join in with some words and phrases when reading familiar simple stories and poems together. **1Ra.03** Read aloud simple texts independently. **1Ra.04** Talk about texts heard or read, including making links with own experiences and expressing likes and dislikes.
Writing	**1Ww.01** Identify the most common letter(s) (grapheme(s)) associated with each sound in the English language. **1Ww.02** Identify letters (graphemes) for adjacent consonants (e.g. *br*, *nd*) and consonant digraphs, including *th*, *ch* and *sh*. **1Ww.03** Relate rhyme to shared spelling patterns, e.g. *rock*, *clock*, *sock*. **1Ww.05** Choose plausible graphemes that match phonemes to write simple regular words and to attempt other words. **1Ww.06** Spell familiar words accurately, including common exception words. **1Wg.01** Use a capital letter and full stop to start and end a sentence. **1Wg.03** Use a capital letter for '*I*', for proper nouns and to start some sentences in more extended writing. **1Wg.04** Write simple sentences. **1Wp.02** Form lower-case and upper-case letters correctly. **1Wp.04** Record answers to simple questions about texts, e.g. in lists.
Speaking and Listening	**1SLm.01** Speak audibly and clearly with familiar people. **1SLm.02** Provide relevant information, as needed. **1SLm.03** Use some relevant vocabulary to describe events and feelings. **1SLm.04** Show some use of non-verbal communication techniques. [Stages 1 and 2]

	1SLm.05 Show some awareness of the listener, e.g. by varying tone to engage them, by responding to their non-verbal cues. [Stages 1 and 2] **1SLs.01** Listen and respond appropriately, including following a sequence of simple instructions. **1SLg.01** Work with others in a group. [Stages 1 and 2] **1SLp.01** Re-read sentences aloud with some fluency and expression. **1SLp.04** Engage in imaginative play, enacting simple characters or situations. **1SLp.05** Make a simple personal statement in a familiar context. **1SLr.01** Talk about own activities, including what they enjoyed.

3 Let's find out	
Texts: *In the Forest* *Animal Coats* *Cats* (non-fiction information texts) *Lion* (simple rhyme) *Foxes* (non-fiction, fact file) *Five Little Ducks* (traditional rhyme)	
Reading	**1Rw.02** Identify the sounds (phonemes) represented by more than one letter (consonant digraphs; vowel digraphs; trigraphs, e.g. 'th', 'sh', 'ch', 'ai', 'ee', 'igh'). **1Rw.03** Blend to identify the sounds represented by adjacent consonants, e.g. 'br', 'nd'. **1Rw.05** Use phonic knowledge to read decodable words. **1Rw.06** Use phonic knowledge to sound out some elements of unfamiliar words. **1Rv.01** Begin to show understanding of words and sentences encountered in reading. **1Rv.02** Use pictures in texts as cues to support understanding of unfamiliar words. **1Rv.05** Explore sounds and words in texts, e.g. rhyming words, rhythm. **1Rg.01** Re-read text showing understanding of capital letters and full stops to indicate sentences, and simple grammatical links between words, e.g. *[The girl] [is playing] with [her ball].* **1Rs.02** Explore and recognise the features of text structure in a range of different fiction and non-fiction texts, including simple poems. [Stages 1 and 2] **1Rs.03** Explore and recognise parts of a book, including cover, title and contents. **1Rs.04** Explore and recognise how texts for different purposes look different, e.g. different uses of pictures. **1Ri.01** Read and explore a range of simple stories and poems, including identifying the contribution of any visual elements. [Stages 1 and 2] **1Ri.03** Read and explore a range of simple non-fiction text types. [Stages 1 and 2] **1Ri.04** Begin to show awareness that different non-fiction text types have different purposes and begin to identify their features. [Stages 1 and 2] **1Ri.05** Explore explicit meanings in simple texts. [Stages 1 and 2] **1Ri.08** Find information by reading labels, lists and captions. **1Ri.12** Respond verbally to simple questions about texts read or heard. **1Ri.14** Show understanding of rhyme and repetition when joining in with reading familiar simple stories and poems. **1Ra.01** Enjoy reading and hearing a range of simple stories, poems and non-fiction texts. [Stages 1 and 2] **1Ra.03** Read aloud simple texts independently.
Writing	**1Ww.02** Identify letters (graphemes) for adjacent consonants (e.g. *br*, *nd*) and consonant digraphs, including *th*, *ch* and *sh*. **1Ww.03** Relate rhyme to shared spelling patterns, e.g. *rock*, *clock*, *sock*. **1Ww.04** Explore and use plural nouns with endings –*s* and –*es*, and understand the effect on the meaning of a noun of adding these endings. **1Ww.05** Choose plausible graphemes that match phonemes to write simple regular words and to attempt other words. **1Ww.06** Spell familiar words accurately, including common exception words. **1Wv.01** Use vocabulary relevant to a familiar topic. [Stages 1 and 2] **1Wg.01** Use a capital letter and full stop to start and end a sentence. **1Wg.04** Write simple sentences. **1Ws.02** Use simple organisational features appropriate to the text type, e.g. subheadings, labelled diagrams. [Stages 1 and 2]

	1Wc.02 Plan writing by speaking aloud, e.g. saying sentences or describing a sequence of events before writing them. **1Wc.04** Begin to write for a purpose using basic language and features appropriate for the text type. [Stages 1 and 2] **1Wp.04** Record answers to simple questions about texts, e.g. in lists. **1Wp.05** Present text in a range of different ways, e.g. diagrams with typed labels, storyboards with handwritten captions. [Stages 1 and 2]
Speaking and Listening	**1SLm.01** Speak audibly and clearly with familiar people. **1SLs.01** Listen and respond appropriately, including following a sequence of simple instructions. **1SLs.02** Ask simple questions about what is heard or read. **1SLg.03** During a discussion, listen to others without interrupting. **1SLg.04** Take turns in speaking, expressing own feelings and ideas. **1SLp.02** Recite simple poems, showing awareness of rhythm.

4 The moon	
Texts: *Bot on the Moon* (fantasy story) *Mister Moon* (poetry)	
Reading	**1Rw.01** Know the name of each letter in the English alphabet and the most common sound (phoneme) associated with it. **1Rw.03** Blend to identify the sounds represented by adjacent consonants, e.g. 'br', 'nd'. **1Rw.05** Use phonic knowledge to read decodable words. **1Rw.06** Use phonic knowledge to sound out some elements of unfamiliar words. **1Rw.07** Begin to recognise a range of common words on sight, including common exception words. **1Rv.01** Begin to show understanding of words and sentences encountered in reading. **1Rv.02** Use pictures in texts as cues to support understanding of unfamiliar words. **1Rv.04** Recite the alphabet in order. **1Rv.05** Explore sounds and words in texts, e.g. rhyming words, rhythm. **1Rg.01** Re-read text showing understanding of capital letters and full stops to indicate sentences, and simple grammatical links between words, e.g. *[The girl] [is playing] with [her ball].* **1Rg.02** Explore in texts, and understand, the use of full stops and different uses of capital letters. **1Rg.03** Identify sentences in texts. **1Rg.04** Explore in texts sentences that contain *and*. **1Rs.01** Talk about the sequence of events or actions in a text, e.g. what happens at the beginning, in the middle and at the end of a story. **1Rs.02** Explore and recognise the features of text structure in a range of different fiction and non-fiction texts, including simple poems. [Stages 1 and 2] **1Rs.03** Explore and recognise parts of a book, including cover, title and contents. **1Ri.01** Read and explore a range of simple stories and poems, including identifying the contribution of any visual elements. [Stages 1 and 2] **1Ri.05** Explore explicit meaning in simple texts. [Stages 1 and 2] **1Ri.06** Retell a familiar story verbally, including most of the relevant information. **1Ri.07** Identify the main characters in a story and talk about what happens to them. **1Ri.08** Find information by reading labels, lists and captions. **1Ri.10** Anticipate what happens next in a story. **1Ri.12** Respond verbally to simple questions about texts read or heard. **1Ri.14** Show understanding of rhyme and repetition when joining in with reading familiar simple stories and poems. **1Ra.01** Enjoy reading and hearing a range of simple stories, poems and non-fiction texts. [Stages 1 and 2] **1Ra.03** Read aloud simple texts independently. **1Ra.04** Talk about texts heard or read, including making links with own experiences and expressing likes and dislikes. **1Ra.05** Begin to make choices about books to read or listen to for pleasure. **1Ra.06** Begin to identify how contexts and events in stories are the same as or different from real life.
Writing	**1Ww.02** Identify letters (graphemes) for adjacent consonants (e.g. *br*, *nd*) and consonant digraphs, including *th*, *ch* and *sh*. **1Ww.03** Relate rhyme to shared spelling patterns, e.g. *rock*, *clock*, *sock*.

	1Ww.05 Choose plausible graphemes that match phonemes to write simple regular words and to attempt other words. **1Ww.06** Spell familiar words accurately, including common exception words. **1Wg.01** Use a capital letter and full stop to start and end a sentence. **1Wg.04** Write simple sentences. **1Ws.01** Develop a simple sequence of known actions or events, e.g. by ordering sentences and then adding to them. **1Wc.03** Develop a short written retelling of a familiar story, e.g. by writing sentences to caption pictures. **1Wc.04** Begin to write for a purpose using basic language and features appropriate for the text type. [Stages 1 and 2] **1Wp.04** Record answers to simple questions about texts, e.g. in lists.
Speaking and Listening	**1SLm.01** Speak audibly and clearly with familiar people. **1SLs.01** Listen and respond appropriately, including following a sequence of simple instructions. **1SLs.02** Ask simple questions about what is heard or read. **1SLg.01** Work with others in a group. [Stages 1 and 2] **1SLg.04** Take turns in speaking, expressing own feelings and ideas. **1SLp.03** Pause at full stops when reading aloud. **1SLp.05** Make a simple personal statement in a familiar context. **1SLr.01** Talk about own activities, including what they enjoyed.

5 *Funny Fish*	
Texts: *Funny Fish* (story with patterned and predictable language) *A Fine Feathered Fish* (nonsense poem) *Nut Tree* (Teacher's Guide only) (rhyming poem)	
Reading	**1Rw.01** Know the name of each letter in the English alphabet and the most common sound (phoneme) associated with it. **1Rw.02** Identify the sounds (phonemes) represented by more than one letter (consonant digraphs; vowel digraphs; trigraphs, e.g. 'th', 'sh', 'ch', 'ai', 'ee', 'igh'). **1Rw.03** Blend to identify the sounds represented by adjacent consonants, e.g. 'br', 'nd'. **1Rw.04** Read verbs with endings *–s*, *–ed*, *–ing*. **1Rw.05** Use phonic knowledge to read decodable words. **1Rw.06** Use phonic knowledge to sound out some elements of unfamiliar words. **1Rw.07** Begin to recognise a range of common words on sight, including common exception words. **1Rv.01** Begin to show understanding of words and sentences encountered in reading. **1Rv.02** Use pictures in texts as cues to support understanding of unfamiliar words. **1Rv.04** Recite the alphabet in order. **1Rv.05** Explore sounds and words in texts, e.g. rhyming words, rhythm. **1Rg.04** Explore in texts sentences that contain *and.* **1Rg.06** Explore in texts examples of nouns and verbs. **1Rs.03** Explore and recognise parts of a book, including cover, title and contents. **1Ri.01** Read and explore a range of simple stories and poems, including identifying the contribution of any visual elements. [Stages 1 and 2] **1Ri.05** Explore explicit meaning in simple texts. [Stages 1 and 2] **1Ri.07** Identify the main characters in a story and talk about what happens to them. **1Ri.10** Anticipate what happens next in a story. **1Ri.11** Make simple inferences based on events in a text. **1Ri.12** Respond verbally to simple questions about texts read or heard. **1Ri.13** Answer questions about text with some explanation of thinking. [Stages 1 and 2] **1Ri.14** Show understanding of rhyme and repetition when joining in with reading familiar simple stories and poems. **1Ra.01** Enjoy reading and hearing a range of simple stories, poems and non-fiction texts. [Stages 1 and 2] **1Ra.02** Join in with some words and phrases when reading familiar simple stories and poems together. **1Ra.03** Read aloud simple texts independently. **1Ra.04** Talk about texts heard or read, including making links with own experiences and expressing likes and dislikes. **1Ra.05** Begin to make choices about books to read or listen to for pleasure.

Introduction

Writing	**1Ww.03** Relate rhyme to shared spelling patterns, e.g. *rock, clock, sock*. **1Ww.06** Spell familiar words accurately, including common exception words. **1Wg.01** Use a capital letter and full stop to start and end a sentence. **1Wg.04** Write simple sentences. **1Ws.02** Use simple organisational features appropriate to the text type, e.g. subheadings, labelled diagrams. [Stages 1 and 2] **1Wc.01** Begin to write simple stories and poems, including using the structures of familiar stories and poems. [Stages 1 and 2] **1Wp.01** Develop a comfortable and efficient pencil grip. **1Wp.02** Form lower-case and upper-case letters correctly.
Speaking and Listening	**1SLm.01** Speak audibly and clearly with familiar people. **1SLm.02** Provide relevant information, as needed. **1SLm.05** Show some awareness of the listener, e.g. by varying tone to engage them, by responding to their non-verbal cues. [Stages 1 and 2] **1SLs.01** Listen and respond appropriately, including following a sequence of simple instructions. **1SLg.01** Work with others in a group. [Stages 1 and 2] **1SLg.02** Show understanding of the opinions of others. [Stages 1 and 2] **1SLg.03** During a discussion, listen to others without interrupting. **1SLg.04** Take turns in speaking, expressing own feelings and ideas. **1SLp.01** Re-read sentences aloud with some fluency and expression. **1SLp.02** Recite simple poems, showing awareness of rhythm. **1SLp.03** Pause at full stops when reading aloud. **1SLr.01** Talk about own activities, including what they enjoyed.

6 Food	
Texts: Pie diagram Poster (non-fiction, labels and headings) *Fish and seafood* *Fruit and vegetables* *Dairy and eggs* *Bread and cereals* *Sugar and fats* (non-fiction texts)	
Reading	**1Rw.03** Blend to identify the sounds represented by adjacent consonants, e.g. 'br', 'nd'. **1Rw.05** Use phonic knowledge to read decodable words. **1Rw.06** Use phonic knowledge to sound out some elements of unfamiliar words. **1Rv.01** Begin to show understanding of words and sentences encountered in reading. **1Rv.02** Use pictures in texts as cues to support understanding of unfamiliar words. **1Rg.01** Re-read text showing understanding of capital letters and full stops to indicate sentences, and simple grammatical links between words, e.g. *[The girl] [is playing] with [her ball].* **1Rg.07** Explore, and understand, the use of articles *the* and *a* or *an* in sentences. **1Ri.03** Read and explore a range of simple non-fiction text types. [Stages 1 and 2] **1Ri.04** Begin to show awareness that different non-fiction text types have different purposes and begin to identify their features. [Stages 1 and 2] **1Ri.05** Explore explicit meaning in simple texts. [Stages 1 and 2] **1Ri.08** Find information by reading labels, lists and captions. **1Ri.12** Respond verbally to simple questions about texts read or heard. **1Ri.13** Answer questions about texts with some explanation of thinking. [Stages 1 and 2]
Writing	**1Ww.03** Relate rhyme to shared spelling patterns, e.g. *rock, clock, sock*. **1Wv.01** Use vocabulary relevant to a familiar topic. [Stages 1 and 2] **1Wg.02** In more extended writing, end some sentences with a full stop. **1Wg.04** Write simple sentences. **1Wg.06** Use articles *the* and *a* or *an* appropriately in sentences. **1Ws.01** Develop a simple sequence of known actions or events, e.g. by ordering sentences and then adding to them. **1Wc.04** Begin to write for a purpose using basic language and features appropriate for the text type. [Stages 1 and 2]

	1Wc.05 Include some relevant information when writing simple non-fiction texts in familiar real-life contexts. **1Wp.04** Record answers to simple questions about texts, e.g. in lists. **1Wp.05** Present text in a range of different ways, e.g. diagrams with typed labels, storyboards with handwritten captions. [Stages 1 and 2]
Speaking and Listening	**1SLm.01** Speak audibly and clearly with familiar people. **1SLm.02** Provide relevant information, as needed. **1SLm.03** Use some relevant vocabulary to describe events and feelings. **1SLm.05** Show some awareness of the listener, e.g. by varying tone to engage them, by responding to their non-verbal cues. [Stages 1 and 2] **1SLg.01** Work with others in a group. [Stages 1 and 2] **1SLg.03** During a discussion, listen to others without interrupting. **1SLg.04** Take turns in speaking, expressing own feelings and ideas. **1SLp.05** Make a simple personal statement in a familiar context.

7 Traditional stories	
Texts: *The Small Bun* (traditional story) *Recipe* (instructions)	
Reading	**1Rw.02** Identify the sounds (phonemes) represented by more than one letter (consonant digraphs; vowel digraphs; trigraphs, e.g. 'th', 'sh', 'ch', 'ai', 'ee', 'igh'). **1Rw.05** Use phonic knowledge to read decodable words. **1Rw.06** Use phonic knowledge to sound out some elements of unfamiliar words. **1Rw.07** Begin to recognise a range of common words on sight, including common exception words. **1Rv.01** Begin to show understanding of words and sentences encountered in reading. **1Rv.02** Use pictures in texts as cues to support understanding of unfamiliar words. **1Rv.03** Identify and record interesting and significant words from texts to inform own writing. [Stages 1 and 2] **1Rg.02** Explore in texts, and understand, the use of full stops and different uses of capital letters. **1Rg.07** Explore, and understand, the use of articles *the* and *a* or *an* in sentences. **1Rs.01** Talk about the sequence of events or actions in a text, e.g. what happens at the beginning, in the middle and at the end of a story. **1Rs.03** Explore and recognise parts of a book, including cover, title and contents. **1Ri.01** Read and explore a range of simple stories and poems, including identifying the contribution of any visual elements. [Stages 1 and 2] **1Ri.02** Identify the characteristics of simple stories. [Stages 1 and 2] **1Ri.03** Read and explore a range of simple non-fiction text types. [Stages 1 and 2] **1Ri.05** Explore explicit meaning in simple texts. [Stages 1 and 2] **1Ri.07** Identify the main characters in a story and talk about what happens to them. **1Ri.09** Explore implicit meanings in simple texts. [Stages 1 and 2] **1Ri.11** Make simple inferences based on events in a text. **1Ri.12** Respond verbally to simple questions about texts read or heard. **1Ra.01** Enjoy reading and hearing a range of simple stories, poems and non-fiction texts. [Stages 1 and 2] **1Ra.03** Read aloud simple texts independently.
Writing	**1Ww.03** Relate rhyme to shared spelling patterns, e.g. *rock*, *clock*, *sock*. **1Ww.07** Ask for support in spelling unfamiliar words and use spelling logs to support future writing. [Stages 1 and 2] **1Wv.02** Begin to use some formulaic language, e.g. *Once upon a time …* **1Wv.03** Use own lists of interesting and significant words to extend the range of vocabulary used in written work. [Stages 1 and 2] **1Wg.02** In more extended writing, end some sentences with a full stop. **1Wg.06** Use articles *the* and *a* or *an* appropriately in sentences. **1Ws.01** Develop a simple sequence of known actions or events, e.g. by ordering sentences and then adding to them. **1Wc.01** Begin to write simple stories and poems, including using the structures of familiar stories and poems. [Stages 1 and 2] **1Wc.04** Begin to write for a purpose using basic language and features appropriate for the text type. [Stages 1 and 2] **1Wp.01** Develop a comfortable and efficient pencil grip.

	1Wp.03 Join some letters, including to support use of multi-letter graphemes. **1Wp.05** Present text in a range of different ways, e.g. diagrams with typed labels, storyboards with handwritten captions. [Stages 1 and 2] **1Wp.06** Read own writing aloud and talk about it.
Speaking and Listening	**1SLm.01** Speak audibly and clearly with familiar people. **1SLs.01** Listen and respond appropriately, including following a sequence of simple instructions. **1SLg.01** Work with others in a group. [Stages 1 and 2] **1SLg.04** Take turns in speaking, expressing own feelings and ideas. **1SLp.01** Re-read sentences aloud with some fluency and expression. **1SLp.03** Pause at full stops when reading aloud. **1SLp.04** Engage in imaginative play, enacting simple characters or situations. **1SLr.02** Suggest how someone's non-verbal communication reflects their feelings.

8 Feelings	
Texts: *The Lonely Penguin* (story with predictable structure and patterned language) *Penguins* (non-fiction fact file)	
Reading	**1Rw.02** Identify the sounds (phonemes) represented by more than one letter (consonant digraphs; vowel digraphs; trigraphs, e.g. 'th', 'sh', 'ch', 'ai', 'ee', 'igh'). **1Rw.04** Read verbs with endings *–s*, *–ed*, *–ing*. **1Rw.06** Use phonic knowledge to sound out some elements of unfamiliar words. **1Rv.01** Begin to show understanding of words and sentences encountered in reading. **1Rv.02** Use pictures in texts as cues to support understanding of unfamiliar words. **1Rv.03** Identify and record interesting and significant words from texts to inform own writing. [Stages 1 and 2] **1Rg.01** Re-read text showing understanding of capital letters and full stops to indicate sentences, and simple grammatical links between words, e.g. *[The girl] [is playing] with [her ball].* **1Rg.02** Explore in texts, and understand, the use of full stops and different uses of capital letters. **1Rg.03** Identify sentences in texts. **1Rg.05** Explore in texts, and understand, the grammar of statements, including the importance of verbs and word order. **1Rg.06** Explore in texts examples of nouns and verbs. **1Rs.01** Talk about the sequence of events or actions in a text, e.g. what happens at the beginning, in the middle and at the end of a story. **1Rs.02** Explore and recognise the features of text structure in a range of different fiction and non-fiction texts, including simple poems. [Stages 1 and 2] **1Rs.03** Explore and recognise parts of a book, including cover, title and contents. **1Ri.01** Read and explore a range of simple stories and poems, including identifying the contribution of any visual elements. [Stages 1 and 2] **1Ri.02** Identify the characteristics of simple stories. [Stages 1 and 2] **1Ri.03** Read and explore a range of simple non-fiction text types. [Stages 1 and 2] **1Ri.05** Explore explicit meaning in simple texts. [Stages 1 and 2] **1Ri.06** Retell a familiar story verbally, including most of the relevant information. **1Ri.09** Explore implicit meanings in simple texts. [Stages 1 and 2] **1Ri.10** Anticipate what happens next in a story. **1Ri.11** Make simple inferences based on events in a text. **1Ri.12** Respond verbally to simple questions about texts read or heard. **1Ri.13** Answer questions about text with some explanation of thinking. [Stages 1 and 2] **1Ra.01** Enjoy reading and hearing a range of simple stories, poems and non-fiction texts. [Stages 1 and 2] **1Ra.03** Read aloud simple texts independently. **1Ra.04** Talk about texts heard or read, including making links with own experiences and expressing likes and dislikes. **1Ra.05** Begin to make choices about books to read or listen to for pleasure. **1Ra.06** Begin to identify how contexts and events in stories are the same as or different from real life.
Writing	**1Ww.03** Relate rhyme to shared spelling patterns, e.g. *rock, clock, sock.* **1Ww.07** Ask for support in spelling unfamiliar words and use spelling logs to support future writing. [Stages 1 and 2]

	1Wv.03 Use own lists of interesting and significant words to extend the range of vocabulary used in written work. [Stages 1 and 2] **1Ws.01** Develop a simple sequence of known actions or events, e.g. by ordering sentences and then adding to them. **1Wc.01** Begin to write simple stories and poems, including using the structures of familiar stories and poems. [Stages 1 and 2] **1Wc.03** Develop a short written retelling of a familiar story, e.g. by writing sentences to caption pictures. **1Wc.04** Begin to write for a purpose using basic language and features appropriate for the text type. [Stages 1 and 2] **1Wc.05** Include some relevant information when writing simple non-fiction texts in familiar real-life contexts. **1Wp.01** Develop a comfortable and efficient pencil grip. **1Wp.03** Join some letters, including to support use of multi-letter graphemes. **1Wp.04** Record answers to simple questions about texts, e.g. in lists. **1Wp.05** Present text in a range of different ways, e.g. diagrams with typed labels, storyboards with handwritten captions. [Stages 1 and 2] **1Wp.06** Read own writing aloud and talk about it.
Speaking and Listening	**1SLm.01** Speak audibly and clearly with familiar people. **1SLm.03** Use some relevant vocabulary to describe events and feelings. **1SLg.01** Work with others in a group. [Stages 1 and 2] **1SLg.02** Show understanding of the opinions of others. [Stages 1 and 2] **1SLg.03** During a discussion, listen to others without interrupting. **1SLg.04** Take turns in speaking, expressing own feelings and ideas. **1SLp.05** Make a simple personal statement in a familiar context. **1SLr.01** Talk about own activities, including what they enjoyed. **1SLr.02** Suggest how someone's non-verbal communication reflects their feelings.

9 Life lessons	
Texts: *Anansi and Turtle* (Traditional African folktale) *Myrtle and Merlin and Micky MacMouse* (Rhyming poem)	
Reading	**1Rw.01** Know the name of each letter in the English alphabet and the most common sound (phoneme) associated with it. **1Rw.02** Identify the sounds (phonemes) represented by more than one letter (consonant digraphs; vowel digraphs; trigraphs, e.g. 'th', 'sh', 'ch', 'ai', 'ee', 'igh'). **1Rw.04** Read verbs with endings *–s*, *–ed*, *–ing*. **1Rw.05** Use phonic knowledge to read decodable words. **1Rw.06** Use phonic knowledge to sound out some elements of unfamiliar words. **1Rv.01** Begin to show understanding of words and sentences encountered in reading. **1Rv.02** Use pictures in texts as cues to support understanding of unfamiliar words. **1Rv.03** Identify and record interesting and significant words from texts to inform own writing. [Stages 1 and 2] **1Rv.04** Recite the alphabet in order. **1Rv.05** Explore sounds and words in texts, e.g. rhyming words, rhythm. **1Rg.02** Explore in texts, and understand, the use of full stops and different uses of capital letters. **1Rg.04** Explore in texts sentences that contain *and*. **1Rg.05** Explore in texts, and understand, the grammar of statements, including the importance of verbs and word order. **1Rg.06** Explore in texts examples of nouns and verbs. **1Ri.01** Read and explore a range of simple stories and poems, including identifying the contribution of any visual elements. [Stages 1 and 2] **1Ri.05** Explore explicit meaning in simple texts. [Stages 1 and 2] **1Ri.06** Retell a familiar story verbally, including most of the relevant information. **1Ri.07** Identify the main characters in a story and talk about what happens to them. **1Ri.09** Explore implicit meanings in simple texts. [Stages 1 and 2] **1Ri.10** Anticipate what happens next in a story. **1Ri.11** Make simple inferences based on events in a text. **1Ri.12** Respond verbally to simple questions about texts read or heard. **1Ri.13** Answer questions about text with some explanation of thinking. [Stages 1 and 2]

Introduction

	1Ri.14 Show understanding of rhyme and repetition when joining in with reading familiar simple stories and poems. **1Ra.01** Enjoy reading and hearing a range of simple stories, poems and non-fiction texts. [Stages 1 and 2] **1Ra.02** Join in with some words and phrases when reading familiar simple stories and poems together. **1Ra.03** Read aloud simple texts independently. **1Ra.04** Talk about texts heard or read, including making links with own experiences and expressing likes and dislikes.
Writing	**1Ww.03** Relate rhyme to shared spelling patterns, e.g. *rock*, *clock*, *sock*. **1Ww.04** Explore and use plural nouns with endings -*s* and -*es*, and understand the effect on the meaning of a noun of adding these endings. **1Wv.03** Use own lists of interesting and significant words to extend the range of vocabulary used in written work. [Stages 1 and 2] **1Wg.01** Use a capital letter and full stop to start and end a sentence. **1Wg.02** In more extended writing, end some sentences with a full stop. **1Wg.03** Use a capital letter for '*I*', for proper nouns and to start some sentences in more extended writing. **1Wg.04** Write simple sentences. **1Wg.05** Use *and* to join words and clauses. **1Ws.01** Develop a simple sequence of known actions or events, e.g. by ordering sentences and then adding to them. **1Wc.01** Begin to write simple stories and poems, including using the structures of familiar stories and poems. [Stages 1 and 2] **1Wc.02** Plan writing by speaking aloud, e.g. saying sentences or describing a sequence of events before writing them. **1Wc.05** Include some relevant information when writing simple non-fiction texts in familiar real-life contexts. **1Wp.02** Form lower-case and upper-case letters correctly. **1Wp.04** Record answers to simple questions about texts, e.g. in lists.
Speaking and Listening	**1SLm.01** Speak audibly and clearly with familiar people. **1SLm.04** Show some use of non-verbal communication techniques. [Stages 1 and 2] **1SLg.01** Work with others in a group. [Stages 1 and 2] **1SLg.02** Show understanding of the opinions of others. [Stages 1 and 2] **1SLg.03** During a discussion, listen to others without interrupting. **1SLg.04** Take turns in speaking, expressing own feelings and ideas. **1SLp.02** Recite simple poems, showing awareness of rhythm. **1SLp.04** Engage in imaginative play, enacting simple characters or situations. **1SLr.02** Suggest how someone's non-verbal communication reflects their feelings.

Note that handwriting is not taught explicitly in this course, although objectives '**1Wp.01** Develop a comfortable and efficient pencil grip', and '**1Wp.02** Form lower-case and upper-case letters correctly', are implicitly covered in the activities and supporting notes in the Teacher's Guide. We recommend that teachers choose a structured and suitable course for teaching handwriting skills at Stage 1 level.

Unit 1 Going places

Unit overview

As learners work through this unit, they will read a story aloud and then retell and talk about the events in the story. *The Big Red Bus* is a simple story with familiar settings. Extracts introduce a non-fiction report. Learners will also read and memorise a simple rhyme. They will learn about the layout of lists and signs before writing their own.

The unit could be part of a study of different types of transport and/or a study of the local area.

Learners will have opportunities to develop hearing and identifying phonemes in words, and to blend and segment phonemes to read and spell words in isolation and embedded in text.

They will have opportunities to read high frequency words and other familiar words.

Introducing the unit

You could introduce this unit by showing learners some pictures of different types of transport, for example bicycles, boats, cars, buses, planes, trains, vans and trucks, leading to a discussion on their similarities and differences. You could then move on to discuss the different means of transport that learners might use, and when they might use each type.

If there is time, put learners in pairs or small groups. Give each learner a different type of transport (a picture of a vehicle or a card with the name of a vehicle on it). Learners should not show each other their cards. Ask them to take turns to describe the type of transport to each other; their partner or group tries to guess what is being described.

Week 1

Key strands and substrands: Lesson outcomes

Reading

- Use pictures and labels to broaden vocabulary and answer questions
- Explore and recognise parts of a book
- Listen to and answer questions about a simple story
- Read a simple story aloud
- Explore explicit meanings and make simple inferences about a simple story
- Use phonic knowledge, including letters of the alphabet, to read decodable words and to sound out elements of unfamiliar words
- Explore the use of 'I' as a capital letter

Writing

- Draw and label pictures using relevant vocabulary
- Record answers to simple questions about texts in lists

Speaking and listening

- Give clear and relevant answers to questions
- Ask questions about a story
- Work with others in a group, listening without interrupting

Resources

- Student's Book pages 1–6
- Workbook pages 1–3
- Slideshows: *Bus poem; The Big Red Bus*
- Audio files: *Bus poem; The Big Red Bus*

The focus this week is on familiarising learners with the format of the Student's Book itself, and with story books and how they work. They will learn to apply a range of strategies for decoding unfamiliar words. They will also join in with reading and complete a range of activities that demonstrate their understanding of what they have read.

Workbook page 1

Vocabulary: transport words

In this activity, learners match the words to the pictures.

Having discussed different types of transport in the introduction, invite learners to look at the pictures and identify each one. Remind learners to use phonic clues to work out words. Only two words begin with the same letter, so initial sounds should help for most words. 'boat' and 'bus' both start with *b* so what should they do to work out what sound comes next? Most learners will recognise 'bus' or be able to sound it out. If not, it is important to help them to use strategies, for example to look for other clues. The word 'bus' ends with *s* and 'boat' ends with *t*. Always encourage learners to look for ways of working out what a word says.

Student's Book page 1

Listening and speaking

Give learners the opportunity to try to read the questions in pairs or on their own before inviting one learner to read them aloud. Model correct reading and ensure that learners understand what is being asked of them, before giving them time to do the activity. Learners should work in pairs and be encouraged to listen to each other without interrupting.

When pairs have had enough time to discuss the questions, bring the class together for a discussion.

Extension: Choose one or more of the topics discussed, for example how learners travel to school. Ask learners to collect data from a suitable number of their peers (at least eight) to answer the question. They can use a table or tallies to do this. Once they have collected the data, ask them to use it to draw a simple pictograph or block graph to display their findings. Make sure they label the graph correctly and that they give it a heading to make its meaning clear. (See the Cambridge Primary Mathematics curriculum framework for more information on this topic if necessary.)

Vocabulary: transport words

1 Check that learners can read the words below the pictures before moving on to the questions in activity 2. Remind learners that pictures can often help them read and understand a word that they are unsure of.

2 Give learners the opportunity to work in pairs to read the questions. Then bring them together to ensure understanding before they do the activity. Refer back to pictures of different types of transport to reinforce learning.

Remind learners to use the picture clues to help them to read the questions by linking them to the labelled pictures in activity 1.

Highlight the question words 'What' and 'How many'. Invite learners to give examples of questions beginning with 'What' and 'How many'. Then ask them to answer each other's questions. For example:

- What is your name?
- What colour is your hair?
- How many feet do you have?
- How many girls are in the class?

3 Give learners some time to draw and label their pictures. Alternatively, they can cut out pictures from newspapers or magazines and use those instead of drawing. Labels could be handwritten or typed.

Answers

2 red; white; two; four

Student's Book page 2

Listening and speaking

Read the poem aloud to the class. The poem is a simple recount of a bus trip. Six friends get on a bus and then get off at the wrong stop.

Spend time with groups or with the class talking about bus trips and let learners recount some of their own experiences briefly. If learners do not often use a bus, talk briefly about trips in other vehicles.

Extension: Ask learners to read the poem aloud in pairs.

Reading and writing

At this point, it would be a good idea to discuss the format of the Student's Book. It may be the first time that learners have used a text book of this style. Point out where the story section is and its format.

Unit 1 • Going places

There are four pages of the story on each page of the Student's Book.

Display the picture of the cover of *The Big Red Bus* on page 2 and spend some time ensuring that learners know the terms 'title' and 'illustrator'. Use other books in the classroom to highlight features such as the title, the author's name and the illustrator's name. (Some books are written and illustrated by the same person.)

Give learners the opportunity to try to read the section by themselves or in pairs before drawing them together to ensure that they can read and understand the questions.

Highlight the 'What' questions. Invite learners to give examples of 'What' questions. For example:

- What is your friend's name?
- What school do you go to?

Ask learners who they think wrote the book. Invite learners to give examples of 'Who' questions. For example:

- Who lives in your house?
- Who is going to the park to play?

Support/Extension: Some learners may give answers orally, while others may write answers.

Answers

The Big Red Bus; It is big and red; a big red bus

Workbook page 2

Reading and writing

In this activity, learners add details to a picture to complete a scene.

Before asking learners to do the activity, discuss where the bus might be going and write some suggestions on the whiteboard. Invite learners in pairs to read and then say what they should add to their pictures. Once learners have completed the task, discuss what else could be added to the picture and/or how the scene might look in their community.

Remind learners of the importance of speaking clearly and of listening to their peers without interrupting.

Extension: Ask learners to draw up a list or table of similarities and differences between the scene shown and what they would see at a bus stop in their own community.

Student's Book pages 2–5

Listening and speaking

1 Before learners do the activity, recap good reading practices with them. Then read the story aloud to the class or play the audio file while they follow and listen.

Remind learners where they should start reading. Ask them to point to the first word and then run their finger along the print in the direction that they should read. Remind them that every word on the page has a spoken word correspondence when they read.

Tell learners that when they are following a text while someone else is reading, they should be reading along 'in their head'. They may need to be prompted occasionally, so ask questions, for example: 'Put your finger on the last word that I read. What is the next word?'

Remember that questioning should be done in such a way that it does not focus attention on learners who need support. Some learners could become anxious and this does not help with their reading.

Tell learners you are going to read the story again. This time, while they listen, they have to think about two things. Refer to the text and ask learners to read the questions and say what they have to listen for. Then ask them to follow as they listen to the audio file or you reading the story again.

2 Spend as much time as necessary on this section to ensure correct decoding of the text and to encourage reading with fluency. Encourage learners to use a variety of strategies, for example phonic skills, picture and context clues, reading on and rereading, to decipher any unknown word.

When all learners have finished reading the story, encourage them to ask each other questions about it to help their understanding.

To help learners recognise words and sentences from the story, write some of the words or sentences on cards and let the learners find these in the story. Then take one or two simple sentences and write them differently. For example: *The bus is slow. I press the bell to get on.* Let the learners compare your sentences with the sentences in the story.

3 Learners can ask their partner 'What' and 'Who' questions about the story after they have read it.

Support: Some learners may need teacher support, individually or as part of a small group, to use these strategies when decoding the text.

Answers

1 Nut Hill; Grandad

Student's Book page 6

Reading and writing

Before turning to the activities on page 6 of the Student's Book and page 3 of the Workbook, ensure that learners understand the text by asking questions. For example:

- Where did the little girl and her dad sit on the bus?
- Who was waiting at the bus stop?
- Why do you think the passengers grab on to the rail?
- Why do you think Grandad is sitting down while he waits for the bus?

Spend some time developing the concepts of 'true' and 'false' with learners before attempting the activities.

When checking answers with learners, encourage them to find the evidence to show why an answer is false. For example, 'The bus is very slow' is a false answer. Learners should refer back to the text to show why, for example 'The bus is fast.' (page 6)

The following activity can be used to develop the concepts of 'true' and 'false'. Make a number of statements and ask learners to say whether each one is true or not. Point out that 'true' means 'correct', and 'false' means 'not correct'. For example:

- Birds can fly.
- Trees have leaves.
- The grass is red.
- A car has wheels.
- A frog can fly.
- 4 + 4 = 7

Examples should relate to the learners' own environment.

Invite learners to make statements; the rest of the class answer 'true' or 'false'.

Extension: Ask learners to write two true and two false statements on cards. This activity could be linked to a topic they are learning about, such as transport, birds or farming, or to mathematics. They can then play a game in small groups. Each learner turns over a card and the person to their left has to say whether it is true or false.

Answers

1 The bus is going to Nut Hill; The bus went past the pond; You press the bell to get off.

2 c words: cap, cot, can; b words: bag, bus, bed; m words: map, mix, man

3 bus; bag; bed

Workbook page 3

Reading and writing

This section assesses learners' decoding of a familiar text and understanding of the story. Learners have to match the beginning of sentences with their endings.

Highlight the word 'I' in the story on pages 10 and 12. Explain the use of a capital letter for 'I'. Note that here 'I' is at the beginning of a sentence, but 'I' always has a capital letter wherever it appears as a word. Write some simple sentences on the whiteboard to show this. For example:

- When I am tired, I go to bed.
- I like dhal.
- In the morning I wash my face.

Answers

1 We sit at the back of the bus.
We grab on to the rail.
The bus is fast.
I press the bell to get off.

Weekly review

Use this rubric to assess learners' progress as they work through the activities this week. You can use the activities suggested beneath the table to follow up on your on-going assessment.

Level	Reading
■	Can read the story with assistance and recognise some sight words, but does not consistently apply strategies for decoding unfamiliar words.
●	Can read the story and recognise sight words but does not consistently apply strategies for decoding unfamiliar words.
▲	Can read the story confidently independently and uses a range of strategies to decode words they do not know.

Support: If possible, set up paired reading sessions using parents, helpers, support staff, buddies or whoever is available to you in your situation. These sessions should be ongoing for as long as you think necessary.

Extension: Give learners the opportunity to read and reread a book independently after you have read it aloud to the class. Some learners may work in pairs to do this.

Week 2

Key strands and substrands: Lesson outcomes

Reading

- Know the sounds that the letters of the alphabet represent and use phonic knowledge to decode words
- Use pictures to support understanding of words
- Show understanding of words encountered in reading
- Retell a familiar story verbally
- Recognise the sequence of events in a story
- Explore and understand the use of capital letters and full stops in texts
- Explore rhyming words and rhythm in text

Writing

- Identify letters associated with each sound
- Record answers in lists
- Develop a simple sequence of events
- Relate rhyme to shared spelling patterns

Speaking and listening

- Speak audibly and provide relevant information

Resources

- Student's Book pages 6–7, 9
- Workbook pages 4–6
- PCMs 1–8: Phonics

The focus of this week's work is retelling the story, identifying and using words from the story, and phonic skills.

While phonic skills should be part of the daily programme at this stage, the activities in this week's work are designed to give further practice in reading and writing consonant-vowel-consonant (CVC) words and in developing the concept of rhyme. Learners need to use knowledge of sounds to read and write CVC words. For this reason, these words are presented in lists rather than in a context, to make sure learners decode them rather than use contextual cues to make a sensible guess what the word is.

Learners should be given daily practice in reading and writing CVC words. For encoding these, magnetic letters can be used initially so that learners only have to focus on finding the letters that correspond to the sounds in a spoken word (for example, *bus*, *hot*, *bed*), not the formation of the letters. Individual whiteboards and pens are a good next step.

Student's Book page 6

Sounds and spelling

1 Recap understanding of initial sounds in words by asking learners to say, show and/or write the initial sound of spoken words. At this time, use words where the initial sound is represented by one letter, for example 'sun', 'book', 'duck', 'man'.

2 Ensure understanding of the concept of writing words in lists. For example, write four words – 'red', 'yellow', 'green' and 'blue' – in a list on the whiteboard. Ask learners what they notice about the words and how they are written. (They are all colours and they are written one below the other.) Explain that a list is a number of connected items or names written consecutively, and usually one below the other.

3 Learners look at the pictures and write the CVC word for each picture. Learners can refer to the list of 'b' words above to check spelling.

Support: Magnetic letters could be used for this activity. These allow learners to focus on choosing the correct letters to spell words without having to think about how to form the letters.

Extension: This is an ideal opportunity to focus on broad writing skills and letter formation. Ask learners to write words using different styles, sizes of letters and colours to decorate them and allude to their meaning. For example, the word 'red' could be written in red pencil, or the word 'big' could be written in letters that are much bigger than the others. Allow for creative use of fonts and for learners to play with computer printing if this is available.

Answers

2

cap	bag	map
cot	bus	mix
can	bed	man

3 bus; bag; bed

Student's Book page 7

Reading and speaking

Before asking learners to retell the story, discuss how the map can help with the retelling of part of the story. Invite learners to read the labels on the map and then to reread the story, individually or in pairs.

A good follow-up to the retelling of the story would be to ask questions about the events in the story. For example:

- What happened at the beginning in the story?
- Where was the bus going to?

What did the little girl and her dad do first when they got on the bus?

- What did they do next?
- Why do you think they had to grab on to the rail?
- What did they do before they got off the bus?
- What did the little girl do after she got off the bus?
- What happened at the end of the story?
- The little girl was going to meet her grandfather. Where do you think the other people were going?

Give learners the opportunity to ask each other questions about events in the story. This will allow you to check that learners understand the concept of a question or if they need more chances to explore it.

Support: Work to support individuals or small groups as needed.

Reading and writing

Before asking learners to complete activities 1 to 3, assess their understanding of the concept of a sentence. Write some simple sentences on the whiteboard, highlighting a capital letter at the beginning and a full stop at the end. For example:

- We walked to school.
- Raj ran to the bus stop.
- Jan climbed the tree.

1–3 In this section learners are asked to read sentences from the story and to choose and write the sentence that comes at the beginning of the story. They then write the rest of the sentences in the correct order.

Answers

2–3 We get on the bus. We sit at the back of the bus. We pass the pond and the clock. Grandad is at the bus stop.

Workbook page 4

Reading and writing

In this section, learners are asked to use words from the story; the words are not embedded in the text.

1 Learners choose and write words that describe the bus.

2 Learners label pictures.

3 Learners complete the sentences.

Remind learners to use clues to work out any unknown words.

Answers

1 red, big

2 top left: clock; top right: duck pond; bottom left: bell; bottom right: bus stop

3 red; stop

Workbook page 5

Sounds and spelling

This activity requires close reading by learners. There is only one letter that is different in each pair of words: the initial consonant, the vowel or the final consonant.

Before turning to page 5, learners should practise reading pairs of words where only one letter is different, for example: 'tin' – 'tan', 'cot' – 'cat', 'lid' – 'did', 'top' – 'hop', 'rug' – 'rub' and 'pet' – 'pen'.

After learners have read a pair of words, ask them which sound (beginning, middle or end) is different in each pair.

PCMs 1–6 give further practice in reading and writing CVC words. They should be used, now or later, for all or some learners as needed.

PCMs 1–3 have a particular focus on reading pairs of words where only one letter is different.

PCMs 4–5 focus on writing CVC words. For PCM 5, accept 'cup' or 'mug' as correct.

PCM 6 focuses on reading CVC words in context.

Answers

bin; bag; zip; hat; jug; cat

Workbook page 6

Reading and writing

1 This activity provides further work on reading CVC words. Once learners have read them, they write them in lists that rhyme.

2 Work with learners to create lists of rhyming words. If necessary, help them with one or two words, highlighting the spelling patterns *–ug*, *–an*, *–et* with only the first letter that represents the initial sound changing.

3 This simple rhyme is based on a traditional Irish nursery rhyme. The complete rhyme is:

Dan, Dan, the funny old man, Washed his face in the frying pan, Combed his hair with the leg of the chair, Dan, Dan, the funny old man.

Read it with learners and have them work out the missing word. Once they have done that, ask them to read and memorise the rhyme so they can recite it. Most learners should manage the four-line complete version.

PCMs 7–8 give further practice in CVC words that rhyme. Use these now or later as needed.

Support: Use PCMs 7–8 to reinforce rhyming words and the spelling of CVC words with learners who are struggling. You may also like to play some word games involving rhyming words. For example:

1 Listen for the rhyme

Stick or draw a picture on the whiteboard. Then say a list of words and ask learners to raise their hand when they hear a word that rhymes with the picture.

- Example 1: 'chair'

Suggested words: 'bear', 'cat', 'garden', 'hair', 'stair', 'tree', 'wear', 'pear', 'stone', 'fair', 'bush', 'bucket', 'where'.

- Example 2: 'zip'.

Suggested words: 'drip', 'run', 'ship', 'lip', 'pie', 'hip', 'ten', 'pip', 'chip', 'go', 'box', 'tip', 'dip', 'lid'.

2 Ask for the rhyming words

Prepare strips with overlapping pairs of rhyming words. For this activity to work, you need pairs of words. Each word must appear in the first sentence of one card and the question of another. For example:

I have jet. Who has pet?
I have pet. Who has met?
I have met. Who has net?
I have net. Who has set?
I have set. Who has jet?

Give each learner a strip and decide who will start. The first learner reads their strip and the learner with the correct word then reads theirs.

Extension: Quicker learners can spend some time making up silly rhymes based on the words they have learned and others they know. They can either do this orally or write (and illustrate) them. For example:

- A fat cat with a hat …
- A fat cat with a hat sat on a mat.
- A hen with a pen …

- A hen with a pen counted to ten.

There is a wide range of CVC word rhyming and spelling activities on the internet.

Dictation: At this level, learners need to develop their writing skills at the same time as they are learning to use sounds to write simple words. Use simple phrases and sentences as class dictation on a regular basis to help develop these skills. To encourage listening and thinking skills, instruct learners first to listen carefully to the phrases and/or sentences with their pencils down. Initially, a phrase/sentence may need to be repeated to help learners to memorise it before they are asked to write it down. Use one or two sentences per day.

For example:

- A red bus.
- A hot pot.
- Ten men.
- A fat hen.
- A dog sat on a mat.
- Ted is in the red bed.
- The man is in a big van.
- The fox sat on the box.
- Jez had a cup and a mug.
- Sam has a pen and a zip.

Answers

2

jug	pan	net
tug	fan	get
hug	man	pet
bug	tan	set
rug	can	met

3 pan

Weekly review

Use this rubric to assess learners' progress as they work through the activities this week. You can use the activities suggested beneath the table to follow up on your on-going assessment.

Level	Reading	Writing
■	Can read consonant-vowel-consonant words. Needs further practice to improve accuracy and speed.	Can write most consonant-vowel-consonant words accurately. Copes well with medial a, o, and e but needs more practice with medial u and medial i.
●	Can read consonant-vowel-consonant words with accuracy.	Can write consonant-vowel-consonant words accurately to dictation. Making good progress in own writing.
▲	Can read consonant-vowel-consonant words with speed and accuracy.	Can write consonant-vowel-consonant words accurately to dictation and in own writing.

Support: Offer ongoing practice in reading CVC words with a focus on individual learner's area of difficulty, such as words with medial vowel 'e' or 'i'. Learners should use any or all of PCMs 1–8 as needed.

Extension: Learners should work in pairs. Each learner should write a list of ten CVC words to include two words for each of the five vowels. Learners then swap lists and read their partner's list, checking for any errors.

Week 3

Key strands and substrands: Lesson outcomes

Reading

- Find information and use pictures as cues to understand signs and captions
- Explore fiction and non-fiction book covers and recognise some features of each
- Recite the alphabet in order and identify vowels
- Talk about a story, link it to own experience and express preferences

Writing

- Present text in different ways, including signs, lists and captions
- Write CVC words

Speaking and listening

- Work with others in a group, taking turns and listening to each other's opinions
- Take part in a role play involving simple characters
- Talk about own activities, expressing what they enjoyed

Resources

- Student's Book pages 8–10
- Workbook pages 7–9
- PCM 9: End of unit task

The focus of this week's work is non-fiction books. It is important to give learners opportunities to explore and investigate a selection of books.

Discuss what makes non-fiction books (factual books or information books) different from fiction books (stories), for example: the layout, photographs, diagrams, signs and captions. A selection of fiction and non-fiction books should be made available for learners to look at. Learners will have the opportunity to record information in lists and to write signs and captions.

In addition to the work on books and texts, the Workbook contains focused activities on the alphabet and on the vowels. The following rhymes/songs will help learners to learn alphabetical order and the sound that each letter has:

The A [name] says ah, [sound]
The A says ah,
Every letter makes a sound,
The A says ah.

The B says buh,
The B says buh,
Every letter makes a sound,
The B says buh.

(and so on through the alphabet)

A B C D E F G [gee]
H I J K L M N O P [pee]
Q R S T U and V [vee]
W X Y and Z [zee]
Now I know my ABC,
Come along and sing with me.

Here is a mnemonic to help learners remember the vowels. It can be used for both the names and the sounds of the alphabet letters.

Angry	elephants	in	orange	underwear
a	**e**	**i**	**o**	**u**

Extension: Learners can make up and illustrate a mnemonic of their own.

Student's Book page 8

Reading and speaking

Before learners do the activities in this section, take opportunities to find and discuss signs in the environment – the classroom, school and/or their local environment – or display a picture of signs.

You could take learners on a 'sign walk' to find signs in and around the school. Use a school camera to take photographs of the signs and display them in the classroom later.

Signs that there may be around the school include: Office; Dining hall; Boys' toilets; Girls' toilets; School entrance; Parking for staff; All visitors must report to the school office.

Ask learners to do activities 1 and 2.

Writing

Discuss how signs are written and why they are written in a certain way. For example, visual impact is important; capital letters are often used; signs need to be bold and uncluttered. Ask learners to suggest reasons for this.

Discuss with learners the difference between a list and continuous text. Ask them when they last wrote lists (they did this when they wrote rhyming words) and show them other lists, for example shopping lists, telephone numbers and lists of names. Model writing a list.

Ask learners to do activities 1 and 2.

Role play

Encourage learners to think about how they might greet each other casually in the playground. Then talk about how they might greet other people, such as teachers, adults, their elders and strangers in shops. Move on to a discussion about shopping in general and how you talk to people who are serving you in various places. Focus on politeness and the need to express or ask for what you want.

Ask learners to think of a time that they got new shoes. Spend some time talking about what a shopkeeper might ask or talk about. For example, the person in a shoe shop might ask about the type of shoe, size and colour the customer wants to look at. They may suggest different shoes or ask the customer if the shoes fit or if they are comfortable. How would the shopkeeper stand/look when speaking to and listening to the customer? The person shopping for shoes might ask/talk about the price, different colours, different sizes and whether the shoes are too small, too big or too tight. Discuss with learners how the shopkeeper's facial expression and/or their stance can make the customer feel.

Help learners to develop their conversations, reminding them to speak audibly and clearly. Invite pairs to perform their role play for the rest of the class.

Student's Book page 9

Reading and writing

1 Before learners do this activity, show them examples of captions, ensuring that they understand that a caption is a short piece of text.

2 Before learners do this activity, ensure that they can identify the pictures.

Support: Alphabet strips should be available for some learners to select graphemes from and/or who need help with orientation of letters.

Answers

1 This is the bookshop.
This is the newsagents.
This is the shoe shop.

2 pen; zip; pan/pot; hat; bat; mug/cup; mop; bed

Student's Book page 10

Reading

1–4 Before learners attempt activities 1–4, spend some time looking at book covers. Discuss types of books (fiction and non-fiction), authors and illustrators. Invite learners to choose which type of book they prefer and why.

Images of covers of non-fiction books could be used here.

Answers

2 The story book is *Best Bird*. It has a cartoon picture on the front and not a photograph.
She wrote *In the Forest*.
You can find out about cats in *Pet Cat, Big Cat*.

Workbook pages 7–8

Reading

Before attempting the activities in this section, learners could repeat the songs and rhymes they have learned to revise the alphabet and vowels.

Answers

1 There are 26 letters in the alphabet.
There are five vowels in the alphabet.
a, e, i, o, u.

2 The missing letters are: d, g, j, l, m, o, p, r, s, v, x, y.

Workbook page 9

Sounds and spelling

This section assesses learners' understanding of vowels. Check the following:

- Can learners hear and identify vowel sounds in the middle of words?

- Can learners write the letters that represent the sounds?

Answers

bag; pot; lid; jug; net; hat; log; zip; sun; ten

Student's Book page 10

Thinking time

If necessary, allow learners to read *The Big Red Bus* again before they discuss why they liked or did not like the book. Encourage learners to relate their own experience of travelling on a bus. Do they like travelling on buses? Why/why not?

Weekly review

Use this rubric to assess learners' progress as they work through the activities this week. You can use the activities suggested beneath the table to follow up on your on-going assessment.

Level	Reading	Listening and Speaking
■	Has some understanding of the difference between a fiction book and a non-fiction book. Can read lists, signs and captions in the context of a book with support.	Engages in imaginative play. With support, can express themself in the roles of different characters.
●	Understands the difference between a fiction book and a non-fiction book. Can read lists, signs and captions in the context of a book with minimal support.	Engages in imaginative play. Takes on the roles of characters.
▲	Understands the difference between a fiction book and a non-fiction book. Can read lists, signs and captions in the context of a book.	Engages in imaginative play. Uses different voices when they take on the roles of characters.

Support: Learners should choose a fiction and a non-fiction book and tell you which is which and how they know.

Extension: Ask learners to choose six books from the class library, three fiction and three non-fiction. They should write the book titles in two lists.

End of unit task

Use PCM 9 to assess whether learners can read and follow instructions and whether they can read sentences and sequence them to retell a familiar story. Observe learners as they work and note who can (or cannot) read and understand the instructions.

Check learners' completed work to make sure the sequence is correct. If this is not possible, ask learners to exchange their sentences with a partner and check and correct each other's work.

Before moving on to the next unit, ask learners to work in small groups and talk about what they liked best in the unit and why. This can give teachers an indication of what types of learning activities different students liked/disliked.

Self-assessment

You will find a self-assessment chart on page 60 of the Workbook. Use this as you complete each unit, asking learners to tick the column that best applies to them. You can look at these to gain a sense of which learners feel they need more help and which are confident with their achievements

Unit 2 Having fun

Unit overview

As learners work through this unit, they will read a story aloud and talk about the events in the story. They will make simple inferences about characters and events to show understanding. *Rev and Dev* is a simple story, written in rhyme, with a familiar setting. The unit could be part of a 'Health and Wellbeing' topic looking at how we can keep ourselves fit and healthy.

Learners will begin to appreciate different aspects of a story's language, for example, rhythm and rhyme. They will have the opportunity to read and write consonant-vowel-consonant (CVC) words, to read and write words where two letters represent one sound, and to use rhyme and relate it to spelling patterns. They will have the opportunity to read and spell high-frequency words and other familiar words. They will also have the opportunity to identify characters and talk about them.

Introducing the unit

The unit could be introduced by having a discussion with learners about what they do to keep themselves healthy. They could also have a discussion about what they think they should do but don't do to keep themselves healthy.

Week 1

Key strands and substrands: Lesson outcomes

Reading

- Recognise features of a book cover
- Read a simple story aloud in pairs and explore explicit information
- Identify the main characters in a story and what they do
- Use pictures as cues for understanding words
- Begin to understand words and sentences and explore sounds and rhyming words
- Read verbs ending with *–ing*
- Respond verbally to simple questions

Writing

- Use knowledge of sounds to write simple words
- Create simple sentences
- Record answers to questions about texts in lists

Speaking and listening

- Discuss sporting activities with a partner, using relevant information and vocabulary
- Listen to a story and answer questions
- Read aloud with fluency and expression

Resources

- Student's Book pages 11–15
- Workbook pages 10–12
- Slideshow: *Rev and Dev*
- Audio file: *Rev and Dev*
- PCM 10: Words ending in *–ing*

Student's Book pages 11–14

Listening and speaking

Give learners the opportunity to try to read the instructions in pairs and then on their own before inviting a learner to read them aloud. Model correct reading and ensure that learners understand what is being asked of them before letting them do the activity.

Bring the class together for a discussion. Check if there is a sport many learners would like to be able to do and that could be arranged at school, for example, some learners might like to learn to play rounders.

Reading and writing

Have a discussion about books and their titles, authors and illustrators, using books that learners are familiar with. Discuss how the cover of a book can tell the reader what the book is about. Using a selection of books, invite learners to say what the books might be about by looking at their covers.

Highlight 'Who' and 'What' questions before learners do the activity. Recap 'What' questions (see Unit 1) by asking questions. For example:

- What is the name of your school?
- What is the name of the road where you live?

Then ask learners some 'Who' questions and elicit that the answer will be a name. For example:

- Who brought you to school today?
- Who drew the picture?
- Who left the door open?

Ask learners to look at the picture of the cover of *Rev and Dev* and discuss what information they can find out from it. For example, the story will be about two characters. What are the character's names? Who is who and how do we know? Use the opportunity to discuss the names of characters in other books that you have read to the learners or they know from home.

Give learners the opportunity to read the questions in pairs or on their own before asking a learner to read them aloud. Ensure that learners understand what is being asked of them before giving them time to do the activity.

Answers

Rev and Dev; Learners' own answers

Reading and listening

1 Read the story to the class (pages 12–14).

Tell learners that you are going to read the story again. This time, while they listen, they need to think about these two questions:

- What does Rev like doing?
- What does Dev like doing?

Ensure that they understand before reading the story again by asking them what they need to think about while they listen to the story.

When learners have listened to the story again, invite them to say what Rev likes doing and what Dev likes doing. Are there things that both Rev and Dev like doing?

Help learners refer to the story to find the evidence from pictures or text for their answers.

Workbook page 10

Reading and writing

Following on from working in pairs to discuss things they can do to get fit and their favourite sports, learners complete a chart about these things. If necessary, teach the words in the chart and explain what rows and columns are in order to make reference to charts simpler. (Rows are horizontal (across) and columns are vertical (up and down).) Talk about the headings for each column and what they should write.

Make sure learners understand how to complete the chart by asking them to point to where they will draw:

- their favourite thing to do at school to keep fit
- their partner's favourite thing to do at home to keep fit.

Student's Book page 15

Reading, speaking and writing

Spend as much time as necessary on this section to ensure correct decoding of the text and to encourage reading with fluency. Encourage learners to use a variety of strategies, for example, phonic skills, picture and context clues, reading on and rereading, to work out any unknown words.

Invite learners to say what strategies helped them most when they were reading the text. Was it the rhythm, the rhyme, the visual impact?

Bring the class together and invite individual learners to read aloud. Learners might like to choose the part they read. Some learners might like to read again before reading aloud.

Observe and listen to learners as they discuss the text and talk about what the characters like doing. Check that they speak clearly and audibly and that they are aware of the listener.

Support: Some learners will need teacher support, individually or as part of a small group, to use these strategies. Support them by voicing the strategies they should use:

- What does the word start with?
- Let's try and sound the word out.
- Look at the picture. Does the picture help?
- Let's try reading from the beginning again.

Be careful not to allow the reader to become frustrated; read along with them and supply any word they are having difficulty with. Then ask them to read the sentence on their own.

Vocabulary: action words

Before asking learners to do activities 1 and 2, spend some time looking at words like 'hop' – 'hopping' and 'run' – 'running'. Ask learners what they notice about the words in each pair.

You could make flashcards for pairs of words, for example, 'sit' and 'sitting'; 'hug' and 'hugging'; 'wag' and 'wagging'; 'dig' and 'digging'; 'pop' and 'popping'. Put the flashcards in random order on the whiteboard and ask learners to put them in pairs: a root word together with the corresponding word + *–ing*. (At this stage, learners are not expected to know terms like 'root word'. The activity is a simple matching one.)

Then ask learners: 'What do you notice about the words in each pair? How are they different from one another?' Learners may notice that the final consonant is doubled in the root word before adding *–ing*. Tell learners that this does not always happen and give examples like 'cook' and 'cooking'. (They will learn more about why this is later.)

Give learners opportunities to add *–ing* to given words, for example 'sleep', and have them say what the new word would be. Write the *–ing* word on the whiteboard, emphasising the *–ing* by circling it or underlining it and saying the letters make the sound '*ing*'.

2 Learners answer the questions about the story verbally.

Answers

2 Dev; Rev; Rev; Dev

Workbook page 11

Reading and writing

Ask learners to work in pairs to read the instructions for activities 1–3. To check understanding, ask one pair to say what they have to do.

Draw learners' attention to activity 3 and remind them that the illustration will help them write what Rev likes to do here.

Draw learners' attention to the heading on this page: *Reading and writing*. These are words that appear regularly and learners should recognise the common word ending *–ing*. At this point, the words are for reading recognition only. (Note: 'Writing' has a different spelling pattern – silent 'w'.)

Give learners some time to do the activities independently, monitoring as they do so.

Answers

1 Dev likes running to get fit.
Dev likes hopping to get fit.
Dev likes hopping on top of box.
Dev likes jogging with a fish on a dish.

2 running; hopping; jogging

3 Learners choose one thing that Rev likes to do from the text.

Workbook page 12

Reading and writing

In this section, learners' decoding of a familiar text is assessed, and their understanding of the story.

Learners match the beginnings of sentences with their endings.

Support: Support learners who may have difficulty with decoding, and assess their understanding of the story.

Answers

1 Rev and Dev like to play in the sun.
Dev can run for fun to get fit.
Rev can hop on a rug.
Dev can jog with a fish on a dish.

2 Rev can run with a cap and a map.
Dev can hop on the top of a box.
Rev can hop with a jug and a mug.
Rev and Dev have fun in the mud in the sun.

Extension: Use PCM 10 to reinforce the use of the ending *–ing.*

Weekly review

Use this rubric to assess learners' progress as they work through the activities this week. You can use the activities suggested beneath the table to follow up on your on-going assessment.

Level	Reading
■	Can read a story and recognise sight words but does not consistently apply strategies for decoding unfamiliar words. With support, making progress.
●	Can read a story and recognise sight words but does not consistently apply strategies for decoding unfamiliar words. Uses context well to work out *–ing* words.
▲	Can read a story confidently on their own and use a range of strategies to decode unfamiliar words. Can read words ending in *–ing* well.

Support: Work with a small group of learners, modelling strategies and inviting learners to suggest strategies to work out unknown words in an appropriate text. Read and reread the text encouraging learners to join in where they can. Then give learners the opportunity to work in pairs to read the text.

Extension: Give learners the opportunity to work in pairs to read unfamiliar texts at an appropriate level. Monitor how they use strategies for reading.

Week 2

Key strands and substrands: Lesson outcomes

Reading

- Recognise high-frequency words
- Explore and show understanding of rhyming words
- Use pictures in text as cues
- Identify sounds represented by more than one letter – 'sh'
- Recite the alphabet

Writing

- Spell high-frequency words accurately
- Relate rhyme to spelling patterns and write CVC words correctly
- Identify the most common letters associated with each sound and for consonant digraphs
- Use a capital letter for proper nouns and form them correctly
- Write simple sentences

Speaking and listening

- Speak clearly and engagingly about a topic to a partner
- Make simple personal statements in a familiar context

Resources

- Student's Book pages 16–18
- Workbook pages 13–14
- Slideshow: *Becky Bee*
- Audio file: *Becky Bee*
- PCM 11: Phonics *–sh*
- PCMs 12–13: Phonics *sh, ch, th, wh*

Student's Book page 16

Spelling: high-frequency words

Take every opportunity to help learners to identify, read and learn to spell words from the list of high-frequency words (see page 7 of this resource), many of which are common exception words. Use the 'look, say, cover, write and check' method as one of your strategies.

Why is 'said' a common exception word? Many sound/letter combinations follow similar rules – for example, 'ai' as in pain, rain, main, train. The same letter combination can be seen in 'said'. Here the letters (grapheme) make an 'e' sound. This makes 'said' a common exception word.

Learners need to get into the habit of looking at words with intent: observing details, highlighting difficult parts and visualising and committing the word to memory. Learners with poor visual memories may need extra support and practice to commit words to memory successfully.

1 Here learners are asked to scan pages of text to find high-frequency words. Tell them that they do not have to read every word on the page; instead they should look for the words in a systematic way. For example: 1) They put a piece of card or a ruler under the first line of text. 2) They move their eyes from left to right and stop and point to an identified word if it appears on that line. 3) They then move the card/ruler to the next line of text and repeat the process.

Give learners practice in this skill before moving to the activity.

(See the Cambridge Primary Mathematics curriculum framework for more information on tally marks, if necessary.)

Support: Learners who struggle with this task could work in pairs to find the words.

As a follow-up, ask learners to practise looking at the words and identifying any tricky part. For example, in 'said' learners might think the vowel sound should be represented by the letter *e*. They should practice writing the words from memory.

2 This activity gives practice in using high-frequency words to complete sentences about Rev and Dev.

Answers

1 said ~~||||~~ / 6
you ~~||||~~ ~~||||~~ 10
with ~~||||~~ 5
the ~~||||~~ // 7

2 for; and; on; my

Student's Book page 17

Speaking and writing

In this section, learners are given an opportunity to talk about different sports. Encourage them to include answers to questions such as:

- Are they team or individual sports?
- Can any of them be both team and individual?
- What equipment is needed?
- Where might they be played?

Bring the class together to discuss the different sports, encouraging them to speak clearly and audibly.

Extension: After a short discussion about safety in sport, for example, wearing appropriate clothing such as helmets in some sports, learners could choose a sport and give a short oral presentation about wearing the correct clothing. Monitor how clearly learners speak and how well they choose words to express themselves.

Sounds and spelling

This section focuses on *g* as a final sound in words, and on rhyming words that end in *–ag*, *–eg* and *–og* and then on *x* as a final sound in words, and on rhyming words that end in *–ix*, *–ax*, *–ox*.

Before learners do the activities, give them some practice in rhyming words by asking questions. For example: 'Who can tell me a word that rhymes with "hat" / "bed" / "fit" / "log" / "mix"?'

Support: For some learners, it may be necessary to say things like: 'I'm thinking of a word that starts with *m* and rhymes with "can".'

Answers

1 leg – peg; bag – wag; log – frog

2 fix – mix – six; wax – tax; box – fox

Workbook page 13

Reading and writing

1 Learners complete the sentences to say if they can or cannot do what is illustrated in the pictures.

2 They are then asked to write about what they can do. Encourage learners to develop their writing – for example: 'I can walk with my dog in the park', 'I can play football with my friends'.

Model writing a sentence on the whiteboard, speaking as you go along, for example: 'I remembered a capital letter at the beginning; I was able to sound that word out; I remembered a full stop at the end.'

Support: Some learners may need support with this activity. Invite learners to say what they can do and scribe, if appropriate.

Extension: Learners could then copy the sentence written for activity 2 and illustrate it for a display on the wall.

Student's Book page 18

Sounds and spelling

This section asks learners to write consonant-vowel-consonant (CVC) words in rhyming pairs. Before learners do the activity, give them some practice in identifying rhyming words. The examples below are oral activities and learners should focus on listening for sounds at the end of words.

Example 1: Write the following rhyme on the whiteboard. Read it aloud, emphasising the rhythm and rhyme. Read again and encourage learners to join in with the reading.

Becky Bee is busy,
As busy as can be.
She buzzes round the bushes
And bangs into a tree.
She bumps poor Boris Beetle
When she bounces on his back,
So Boris Beetle beetles off
And hides beneath a sack.

by Joyce Vallar

Ask learners which words rhyme in the poem ('be' and 'tree'; 'back' and 'sack'). You could also take the opportunity to discuss alliteration using the poem as an example.

Example 2: Ask learners which two words sound the same at the end – in other words, which words rhyme.

Suggested words:

- 'flag', 'bag', 'box'
- 'three', 'flower', 'bee'
- 'goat', 'clock', 'sock'
- 'big', 'dig', 'path'
- 'fire', 'tyre', 'book'
- 'meat', 'seat', 'bench'
- 'car', 'house', 'jar'.

Remind learners that the rhyming words in the activity must sound the same at the end; when they write the words, only the first letter of each pair will be different, for example, 'bat' and 'hat'.

Note: 'Rhymes' and 'rimes' are not the same thing. Rhymes have word endings which sound the same but are not necessarily spelled in the same way, for example, 'socks' and 'fox'. Rimes are word endings which always retain the same spelling pattern, for example, 'box' and 'fox'.

Answers

hat – cat; bin – pin; hut – nut; frog – log

Writing

The focus of this section is the use of capital letters at the beginning of names.

1 Learners are asked to write a list of the names of six people in the class. Remind them that the names need to be written in a list. Recap, if necessary, how to write a list.

2 Recite the alphabet with learners. Point out that the alphabet here is written in capital letters. Learners find the letter that begins their own name and identify where in the alphabet it comes.

Extension: Learners could write other names, such as the days of the week or months of the year, names of cities or countries, forming the letters correctly and using a capital letter at the beginning of each name.

Workbook page 14

Sounds and spelling

In this section, learners write consonant-vowel-consonant (CVC) words and then write the words in rhyming pairs.

'Shop' and 'ship' are included on this page and it is necessary to have a teaching session about *sh* before learners do the activities. Tell learners to listen to the words 'shop' and 'ship' and say what sounds they hear in each word (*sh-o-p* and *sh-i-p*). **Note:** There are four letters in each word but only three sounds.

Tell learners that sometimes two letters join together to make one sound: *s* (the name of the letter) and *h* (the name of the letter) join together to make the sound *sh*. Show learners how to write *sh* and write the word 'shop' on the whiteboard. Do the same for the word 'ship'.

Ask learners to tell you words that begin with *sh*. Suggest a few words if necessary, for example, 'shoe' and 'shell'.

Move on to say pairs of words. Learners have to listen very carefully because the sounds at the beginning can sound alike. For example: 'Which words start with *sh*: "shoe" or "sock" / "soup" or "shop" / "shell" or "sell"?'

Tell learners that *sh* is not always found at the beginning of words. Ask them where they hear *sh* in words like 'dish', 'fish' and 'wash'. Give learners practice in identifying where they hear the *sh* sound: at the beginning or end of a word.

Suggested words: 'shop', 'fish', 'shed', 'wish', 'wash', 'shelf', 'shadow', 'shift', 'dish', 'rush'.

Use PCM 11 to reinforce learning.

Extension: Learners could illustrate some phrases. For example:

- a jug and a mug
- a fox on a box
- a hen in a shed
- a fish on a dish.

Alternatively, they could write their own phrases and illustrate them.

Answers

1 mug/cup; ten; shop; pen; mop; zip; jug; ship

2 mug and jug; ten and pen; shop and mop; zip and ship

Dictation: At this level, learners need to develop their writing skills at the same time as they learn to use sounds to write simple words. Use the phrases and sentences below as class dictation to help them develop these skills on a regular basis. To encourage listening and thinking skills, instruct learners to listen carefully with their pencils down. Initially, it may be necessary to repeat the phrase to help learners to memorise it before asking them to write it down. Use one or two phrases or sentences a day to reinforce the skills.

- A fat cat on a mat.
- A jug and a mug.
- A fox on a box.
- A pin in a tin.
- A hen in a shed.
- A hat in a shop.
- A fish on a dish.

Extension: Learners could illustrate some phrases. Learners working at a higher level could write their own phrases and illustrate them.

You may now wish to teach the class some more combinations of two letters making one sound – *ch*, *th* and *wh* – using the same strategies. Use PCMs 12–13 to do this.

Weekly review

Use this rubric to assess learners' progress as they work through the activities this week. You can use the activities suggested beneath the table to follow up on your on-going assessment.

Level	Reading	Writing
■	Can read consonant-vowel-consonant words and words with *sh* at the beginning/end when words are in lists but needs some support when words are in context.	Can write consonant-vowel-consonant words and making good progress with medial *e* and medial *i* in words. Can write words with *sh* at the beginning.
●	Can read consonant-vowel-consonant words and words with *sh* at the beginning/end with accuracy.	Can write consonant-vowel-consonant words and words with *sh* at the beginning/end.
▲	Can read consonant-vowel-consonant words and words with *sh* at the beginning/end with speed and accuracy.	Can write consonant-vowel-consonant words, and words with *sh* at the beginning/end with accuracy.

Support: Learners should choose a phrase from a selection, read it and then illustrate it. For example:

- a fish on a dish
- a brush in a shop
- a shell on a shelf.

Extension: Learners should write a phrase, for example, 'a fish on a dish' (words with *sh)* and illustrate it.

Week 3

Key strands and substrands: Lesson outcomes

Reading

- Read and compare stories, joining in with familiar words
- Find rhyming words
- Identify sounds represented by more than one letter (sh) and use knowledge to decode words
- Recite the alphabet and understand the relationship between upper- and lower-case letters
- Talk about stories, making links with own experiences
- Explore sentences that contain 'and'

Writing

- Record answers in lists
- Identify letters for adjacent consonants ('sh')
- Relate rhyme to shared spelling patterns

Speaking and listening

- Perform a verse from a story with clarity, gesture and expression
- Express ideas about characters' feelings
- Make a simple personal statement in a familiar context
- Talk about personal activities, expressing preferences

Resources

- Student's Book pages 19–20
- Workbook pages 15–17
- Slideshows: *The Big Red Bus, Rev and Dev*
- Audio files: *The Big Red Bus, Rev and Dev*
- PCM 14 End of unit task

Workbook page 15

The alphabet

Invite the class, groups and/or individuals to recite the alphabet. Refer to the Unit 1 alphabet activities and use as appropriate.

Before learners do activities 1 and 2, give them opportunities to practise writing capital letters using dictation. Alphabet strips, with direction markings, should be available to help with orientation of letters.

Remind learners that the alphabet can be written with capital letters and with lower-case (small) letters. Give some examples: *D – d, F – f, W – w*, saying 'capital/small' as you write. Point out that some capitals are the same shape as the small letters, only bigger. For example: *C – c, O – o, P – p, S – s, V – v, W – w, X – x, Y – y* and *Z – z*.

Let learners read the instructions on their own. Check that they understand what is being asked before they do the activities independently.

Answers

1 T, D, F, G, P, B, N, H, M, B, R, S, W, Z

Student's Book page 19

Reading and speaking

This section focuses on two stories, *The Big Red Bus* and *Rev and Dev* and how they are written.

The Big Red Bus is a simple story written in short sentences with no rhyming structure. *Rev and Dev* is a simple story written in rhyme and with some repetition.

Learners are asked to read both stories again, then to work in pairs to discuss the different ways that the stories are written, before bringing everyone together for a discussion.

Reading and writing

1 Here learners are asked to find rhyming words and write them in lists.

It is important that learners are shown how to do this activity in a systematic way. Learners should read page 3 and then write the rhyming words on that page before reading page 5 to find rhyming words. For example, 'Read page 3 and write the rhyming words.'

run fit
fun sit
sun bit

'Read page 5 and write the rhyming words' and so on.

It may be appropriate for learners to complete this activity over two sessions.

2–3 Learners are asked to read sentences about Rev and Dev and then to write the sentence that Rev said.

Support: Some learners may want to refer back to the story to check their answer.

Answers

1 Page 3: run, fun, sun / fit, sit, bit
Page 5: run, fun, sun / cap, map / bag, rag
Page 7: hop, top / bit, fit, sit
Page 9: bit, fit / rug, jug, mug
Page 11: jog, frog / fish, dish / mud, thud

2 I can hop on a rug with a jug and a mug.

Workbook page 16

Sounds and spelling

Remind learners that Rev liked carrying two things at the same time: Rev liked carrying a cap and a map; a bag and a rag; a jug and a mug. Direct learners to pages 13 and 14 and invite them to find the phrases.

1 Write the word 'and' on the whiteboard and ask learners to say two things they like doing using 'and' in a sentence. For example:

- I like running and jumping.
- I have a brother and a sister.

Learners write the word 'and' three times.

2 Here learners are asked to add initial sounds to 'and' to make new words.

Write *at* on the whiteboard. Tell learners that you want to write the word 'cat' and ask them what sound must go at the beginning of *at* to change it into 'cat'. Confirm that it is *c* and write *c* to complete the word. Repeat this for other words, for example: 'sat', 'mat', 'rat', 'fat', 'bat', 'hat' and 'pat'.

Write 'and' on the whiteboard and ask learners what sound is needed to change 'and' to 'hand'. Confirm *h* and complete the word. Then learners do activity 2.

3 Learners add initial sounds to '–end' to make new words.

When learners have finished, ask them what they notice about the words. The words have shared spelling patterns *–and*, *–end*.

Answers

2 band; hand; land; sand

3 send; bend; lend; mend

Workbook page 17

Sounds and spelling

This section focuses on two letters making one sound *–sh*.

1 Give learners opportunities to practise identifying the *sh* sound in words.

Ask learners to listen for the *sh* sound as you say 'fish' and 'dish'. Ask:

- Is *sh* at the beginning of the word?
- Is *sh* at the end of the word?

Do the same with other words, for example: 'shin', 'ship', 'sheep', 'shallow', 'shore', 'shed', 'crash', 'mash', 'wash', 'wish' and 'smash'.

Ask learners to write the letters *sh* a number of times with speed and accuracy to reinforce the pattern.

2–3 Check that learners know what to do in activities 2–3 and then ask them to do the activities.

Answers

2 shop, shed, shut, ship, shell have a *sh* sound at the beginning; dish, wish, rush, mash, fish, rash, hush have a *sh* sound at the end

3 fish; shell; ship

Student's Book page 20

Reading and writing

In this section, learners need to identify words ending in *sh* and then write a list of rhyming words.

Ask learners to do activities 1 and 2.

Support: Encourage learners to make a set of illustrated flashcards to show the meanings of the different words, for example, 'cash' in bold writing, and a few coins. Ask them to underline the *sh* sound in a different colour.

Answers

1 fish; dish

2 cash, mash, rash; fish, wish, dish; rush, hush, mush

Role play

One learner takes the role of one of the characters and says, "Show me, show me what can you do?" Encourage the use of facial expression and gesture. The other learner responds by reciting a verse with expression. Invite pairs to perform for the rest of the class.

Extension: Some learners could develop a different scenario for Rev and Dev and role-play it.

Listening and speaking

Put learners in pairs and ask them to discuss:

- How the story is written and what makes it different from *The Big Red Bus*.
- How did Rev and Dev change towards each other at the end of the story?

Then bring the class together and invite them to say what they have discussed in pairs.

Thinking time

Learners should discuss what they like and don't like about exercise, and what types of exercise they prefer. Encourage learners to give reasons why they prefer one type of exercise over another.

Weekly review

Use this rubric to assess learners' progress as they work through the activities this week. You can use the activities suggested beneath the table to follow up on your on-going assessment.

Level	Listening and speaking
■	Speaks well when enacting simple characters in role play to the class. Should now think about looking more at their audience.
●	Shows awareness of their audience and speaks well to the class when enacting simple characters in role play.
▲	Shows awareness of audience, speaks confidently and shows some use of facial expression and gesture when enacting simple characters in role play to the class.

Support: Give learners practice in reciting any short rhyme of their choice, encouraging them to look at their audience.

Extension: Learners should develop a different scenario for Rev and Dev and role-play it.

End of unit task

Use PCM 14 to assess whether learners can read and follow instructions, and whether they can read sentences and sequence them to retell a familiar story. This activity is similar to the one completed at the end of Unit 1. Focus particularly on those learners who had difficulty reading and following instructions to make sure they can read and understand them this time round. Also check that learners who sequenced work incorrectly show some improvement this time. Record your observations, as necessary.

Unit 3 Let's find out

Unit overview

The focus in this unit is on non-fiction books and information texts. Learners will learn to 'read' the covers of books (illustrations and titles) and to find out if a book might contain information they need.

Learners will have the opportunity to find information from both illustrations and text – lists, labels, signs and captions. They will also have the opportunity to join in with reciting rhymes and playing with language.

Introducing the unit

The unit could be introduced by discussing with learners how they can find different types of information. For example, how could they find out about ocean pollution, whales, natural disasters or local weather conditions?

Explain to learners that the internet allows most types of information to be stored and found online. However, when they cannot use the internet or the information is not clear enough, they may need to use other sources of information, for example the people around them, newspapers, magazines and books. Ask learners to give examples of other sources of information, for example train/bus timetables, platform information, recipe books, store directories and local maps.

Show learners images or display different sources of information (use the examples above as a starting point) and talk about who might use each type of information, why they would use it and when they might need it. Also talk about what problems might result if they cannot find the information they need.

Week 1

Key strands and substrands: Lesson outcomes

Reading

- Explore parts of non-fiction books and notice how they are different from fiction
- Read non-fiction and explore its features
- Use pictures to help understand unfamiliar words
- Start to understand words encountered in reading
- Identify the sounds represented by two letters: ck, ng
- Use phonic knowledge to read and sound out unfamiliar words

Writing

- Write simple sentences, using capital letters, full stops and relevant vocabulary
- Label pictures
- Identify adjacent consonants and relate rhyme to shared spelling patterns
- Choose plausible graphemes that match phonemes to write simple regular words
- Plan writing by speaking aloud

Speaking and listening

- Discuss books with a partner, listening and responding appropriately
- Ask and answer questions

Resources

- Student's Book pages 21–23
- Workbook pages 18–19
- PCM 15: Phonics *ng*
- PCM 16: Phonics *ck*

Student's Book page 21

Listening and speaking

Before learners start the unit, use a selection of non-fiction books to talk about how the front cover of a book can tell the reader what the book is about. Discuss with learners what kind of books they are (non-fiction books), and that this kind of book is sometimes referred to as a factual or information book. Using a selection of non-fiction books, invite learners to suggest what they are about, for example books about animals, transport, dinosaurs, a visit to the dentist, the doctor, the beach, and so on. Invite learners to say what makes them think a book about transport, for example, is a non-fiction book and not a book about an exciting journey on a train.

Then suggest a topic that you want to find out about, for example different types of fruit, and ask a learner to choose a book that they think would be good for finding out about fruit. Discuss their choice and why or why not it would be suitable. Repeat this for other topics, choosing topics to suit the non-fiction books that are available in the classroom.

Before learners do the activity in this section, ask them to read the instructions and questions in pairs.

Highlight 'What' and 'Which' question words and ensure that learners know what is being asked of them. ('What' is used to ask about things or activities; 'Which' is used to ask someone to choose between a small number of options.)

Give learners time to work in pairs and to ask and answer questions. Remind them to take turns to speak, and to listen carefully to what their partner is saying. Monitor while learners work in pairs before bringing the class together to check answers.

Reading and writing

Ensure that learners understand the activities in this section. They should be able to work out that they need to write the titles of the books shown. Make a selection of non-fiction books available in class for the second activity.

Answers

1 *In the Forest*; *Animal Coats*; *Pet Cat, Big Cat*

2 Learners' own answers

Workbook page 18

Writing

Before learners do the activity, show them front covers of non-fiction books to start a discussion about titles. Titles of non-fiction books are often short – sometimes only one or two words, such as 'ROBOTS' or 'Top Dinosaurs'. Discuss the size and style of the print and the use of capital letters.

Then refer to some non-fiction books from the class library and invite learners to comment on how the titles are written. Make sure that all learners can look at the books so that they can get ideas from them.

Now ask learners to work individually to write titles for the books on Workbook page 18.

Student's Book page 22

Reading and speaking

Recap what information a reader can get from the pictures in a book.

1–2 Draw learners' attention to the pictures from the book and give them time to look at them carefully. Encourage them to look for detail.

Write words like 'beak', 'wings', 'webbed feet' and 'feathers' on the whiteboard. Learners then work in pairs to talk about the page of *Animal Coats* shown on Student's Book page 22.

Reading and writing

Learners can now use the information that they found out from the picture, text and discussion to do activities 1 and 2. Remind them to use a capital letter, a full stop and a piece of information about ducks in each sentence. Invite learners to say sentences and write one or two on the whiteboard to demonstrate.

Student's Book page 23

Sounds and spelling

Use the sentence 'A duck has wings' to highlight words where two letters make one sound: *ng* in 'wings' and *ck* in 'duck'.

Focus on *ng* first and remind learners that sometimes two letters join together to make one sound: *ng*. Tell them that *ng* is a nasal sound and that words in English do not start with *ng*, but that *ng* often comes at the end of words.

Ask learners to tell you words with *ng* at the end. Write the words on pieces of paper/card and stick them on the whiteboard, for example: 'song', 'hang', 'sing', 'lung'. Draw learners' attention to the fact that the words all have different vowels and *ng* at the end. Ask them to select words with the *–ing* rhyme from the words on the whiteboard and put them in a list so that the rhyme/spelling pattern is easily seen. Then ask learners to read the *–ing* words.

Learners repeat the procedure to find rhymes with *ang* and *ong*.

Dictate words with *ang* and *ong* for learners to write.

Suggested words: 'king', 'bang', 'gang', 'fang', 'gong', 'ring', 'hang', 'sang', 'sing', 'song', 'wing', 'rang', 'ding', 'dong', 'thing'

Use PCM 15 at this stage to reinforce the phonics work around the *ng* sound.

Repeat the procedure for the sound represented by *ck*.

Suggested words: 'kick', 'rack', 'lick', 'pick', 'back', 'sack', 'sick', 'tick', 'tack', 'pack', 'dock', 'suck', 'neck', 'lock', 'deck', 'duck', 'luck', 'peck', 'rock', 'sock'.

Use PCM 16 at this stage to reinforce the phonics work around the *ck* sound.

Learners do the activities on page 23 in the Student's Book once they have mastered the sounds represented by *ng* and *ck*.

1–2 Learners look at the pictures, say the words for each picture and write the words with *ng* at the end. They then write three rhyming words ending in *–ing*.

3–4 Learners look at the pictures, say the words for each picture and write the words with *ck* at the end. They then write lists of rhyming words ending in *–ock, –uck* and *–ack*.

Answers

1 wing; king; ring

2 ding; sing; ping

3 duck; sock; sack

4 dock, lock, rock; luck, suck, tuck; back, rack, pack

Workbook page 19

Sounds and spelling

This section gives further practice in writing words with *–ng* or *–ck* at the end.

These sentences can be used for dictation in this unit:

- Mum has a ring.
- My sock is on the bed.
- I can pack my bag.
- I sang a song.
- The sack is on my back.

Answers

sock; sing; track; crack; truck; gong; swing; lock; ring

Weekly review

Use this rubric to assess learners' progress as they work through the activities this week. You can use the activities suggested beneath the table to follow up on your on-going assessment.

Level	Reading	Writing
■	Can use pictures and, with support, text to find information. Making good progress at reading words ending in *–ck* and words ending in *–ng.*	Can spell words ending in *–ck* and words ending in *–ng* when words are dictated in a rhyming pattern.
●	Can use pictures and text to find information. Can read words ending in *–ck* and words ending in *–ng.*	Can spell words ending in *–ck* and *–ng* when words are dictated individually.
▲	Can use pictures and text to find information. They can confidently read words ending in *–ck* and words ending in *–ng.*	Can spell words ending in *–ck* and *–ng* when words are dictated individually.

Support: Learners should practice writing words ending in *–ck* or *–ng* through a stepped process:

1 Write only the endings *–ck* or *–ng* to dictated words, for example: lock (ck), ring (ng).

2 Write dictated words ending in *–ck* or *–ng* where the vowel sound is the same, for example: back, sang; dock, long.

3 Write dictated words ending in *–ck* or*–ng* where the vowel sounds and the endings are mixed, for example: luck, ring, neck, bang, sock, song.

Extension: Learners could investigate, read and spell words ending in *–ss, –ff* and *–ll*. They need to know the rule that consonant-vowel-consonant words do not end in *–s*, *–f* or *–l*, with the exceptions of 'gas', 'bus', 'has' and 'his'. (Note: The *s* in 'has' and 'his' sounds like *z*.)

Suggested words: 'mess', 'kiss', 'pass', 'toss', 'boss', 'less', 'miss', 'lass', 'loss', 'moss', 'hiss', 'mass', 'doll', 'cuff', 'bell', 'till', 'pill', 'huff', 'fell', 'bill', 'will', 'muff', 'tell', 'fill', 'ill', 'puff', 'sell', 'hill', 'well'.

Week 2

Key strands and substrands: Lesson outcomes

Reading

- Read non-fiction and explore its features
- Explore contents pages as a feature of non-fiction structure
- Find explicit information in a fact file
- Use pictures as cues to support understanding of unfamiliar words
- Recognise that capital letters and full stops indicate sentences

Writing

- Write simple sentences using capital letters and full stops
- Use vocabulary and organisational features appropriate for a topic and text type
- Record answers to simple questions

Speaking and listening

- Work well in groups, listening without interrupting

Resources

- Student's Book pages 24–27
- Workbook pages 20–21
- Slideshow: *Fact file: Foxes*
- Audio files: *Fact file: Foxes*

Student's Book page 24

Reading, speaking and writing

The focus of this section is getting information from pictures and using it for a purpose. Learners are asked to write a sentence about a deer, foxes, a bat and an owl.

1 Here learners are asked to think what animals would be found in a forest. Bring the class together to clarify if the animals suggested would be found in a forest.

2 Here learners are asked to draw and label a forest animal. Before learners do the activity, talk to them about how to label a picture: the label should be close to the part of the animal that they are naming. Demonstrate with a drawing of your choice.

3 Learners work in pairs to discuss the information they can get from pictures of four forest animals. Monitor how learners take turns to speak and listen to their partner.

4 Before learners do activity 4, discuss the information that learners got from the pictures in activity 3 and write key words/phrases on the whiteboard. Using an owl as an example, write 'fly', 'wings', 'beak', 'nocturnal' and 'eyes at the front of the face'.

Model writing a sentence about a deer, a fox, a bat or an owl before asking learners to think about the sentences they could write. Invite some learners to say the sentence they want to write. Before learners write, ask them what they must remember when writing a sentence.

Student's Book page 25

Reading and writing

Before learners turn to page 25, show them contents pages from a few non-fiction books from the class library. Then show them a contents page and demonstrate how it is used.

Take this opportunity to help learners recognise full sentences. Write a few of the entries on the board and ask: 'Are these sentences?' The learners may say yes because they start with capital letters. Point out that there are no full stops and no complete sentences.

Highlight that, unlike story books, non-fiction books do not need to be read from beginning to end and discuss why this is the case. Explain that a contents page can help the reader to find specific information without them having to read the whole book. For example:

- What would you find out about on page 12?
- What would you find out about on page 8?

1–2 Now ask learners to read the instructions and look at the contents page in activity 1 in the Student's Book. They then answer the questions in activity 2.

Answers

2 page 4; page 10; foxes in the city; a fox's home

Student's Book page 26

Reading and speaking

Ask learners to work in pairs and give them time to read the fact file. Encourage them to look at the illustrations and to get as much information as possible from them before reading the text. Remind them that using information from illustrations along with other strategies, for example initial sounds, can help them to work out unknown words.

Support: Support learners who may find the decoding more difficult by looking at the pictures with them and showing how the pictures can help with reading. For example, ask learners to look at the pictures of the food that foxes like to eat. Then ask them to identify the 'foods' and ask them what sound 'worm' starts with. Ask learners if they can find the word that says 'worms' (the word that starts with *w*) in the section of text about what foxes like to eat. Use the other pictures in a similar way to help learners to read the text.

Bring the class together to read the text, inviting some learners to read aloud. Then discuss what learners have found out about foxes. Ask some questions, for example:

- Where do foxes live?
- When do foxes go out?
- What is a baby fox called?
- What do foxes eat?

Workbook page 20

Reading and writing

Discuss with learners what a fox looks like (they can refer to previous pictures) and elicit the words that are needed to do the activity – ask learners to point to the words in the box.

Tell learners that when they label the parts of the fox, they need to write the name of the animal part in the box that has a line to that particular part.

Student's Book page 27

Reading and writing

1 Ask learners to read the fact file about foxes on page 26 again before they answer the questions. Check that all learners can read and understand the questions.

2–4 Before learners do activities 2, 3 and 4 discuss different ways of finding out information, for example: by looking in books, magazines and leaflets; by watching factual programmes on television; by looking at maps and timetables; by searching for information on the internet; or just by asking someone. It is important to have some of these sources of information available to show what information can be found and where, for example what time a train leaves the station or what different types of bicycles are available in a certain shop.

Ask learners where they could look to find out what young animals are called and help them to find the answers.

Answers

1 a den; (any three of the following) berries, worms, spiders, mice, birds; from bins; a cub

3 camel – calf; sheep – lamb; tiger – cub

4 A baby tiger is called a cub.

Workbook page 21

Reading

Before asking learners to do the activity, discuss with them what a fox, an owl, a snake and a deer look like. Discuss similarities and differences.

Show learners how to 'read' the chart. Tell learners to do the following:

- Read the words in the top row – the names of the animals.
- Read the words down the left-hand side (in the left column) – the names of animals' parts.
- Starting with 'fox', read the words going down on the left and stop when you come to a part that a fox has, in other words, 'legs'.
- Continue to read the words. 'Does a fox have feathers? Antlers? A tail?'

Then choose another animal and work together with learners to check that they know what to do.

Support: Some learners may need support to coordinate reading along the top row and down the left-hand column. A piece of card placed so that learners can only read about the fox will help here. Help learners to position the card and then to move it along when they are ready to read about the owl, and so on.

Extension: Ask pairs of learners to open the Student's Book at page 26 and the Workbook at pages 20–21. Invite them to discuss the different ways the information is presented. The learners have helped to create ways of presenting non-fiction text on pages 20 and 21 of the Workbook. Bring learners together to discuss the differences and benefits, if any, of one type of presentation. You could recap the other type of non-fiction text in Unit 3, the contents page.

Answers

Legs: fox, owl, deer; Feathers: owl; Antlers: deer; Tail: fox, owl, snake, deer

Weekly review

Use this rubric to assess learners' progress as they work through the activities this week. You can use the activities suggested beneath the table to follow up on your on-going assessment.

Level	Reading
■	Can record answers to questions and label a drawing when they have help with organisational skills.
●	Can record answers to questions and label a drawing with minimal support.
▲	Can confidently record answers to questions and label a drawing accurately.

Support: Take time to discuss with learners what they should draw from a given set of labels.

Extension: Learners draw a picture that suits given labels. They label the picture they have drawn. For example:

- roof, door, windows, wall
- roots, stem, flower, leaf
- pedals, handlebars, saddle, wheels

Week 3

Key strands and substrands: Lesson outcomes

Reading

- Find information by reading labels
- Read and enjoy a simple poem and show understanding of features including rhyme
- Explore sound words and show understanding of rhyme in a poem
- Use pictures to work out unfamiliar words
- Show understanding of words encountered in reading

Writing

- Use pictures and labels to write simple sentences with capital letters and full stops
- Record answers to questions in lists
- Write captions
- Relate rhyme to spelling patterns
- Explore and use plural nouns with endings *–s*
- Plan written sentences by speaking aloud
- Start to write a fact file using appropriate language and features

Speaking and listening

- Listen to a poem to find the rhyming words
- Recite a simple poem showing awareness of rhythm

Resources

- Student's Book pages 28–30
- Workbook pages 22–23
- Slideshows: *Five Little Ducks; Lion*
- Audio files: *Five little ducks; Lion*
- PCM 17: Plurals
- PCM 18: End of unit task

Student's Book page 28

Reading and writing

1 In this activity learners need to use information from photographs with labels to write three sentences about cats.

Before learners write the sentences, discuss the pictures and what information learners can get from them. Ask a learner to read question 2. Discuss what is meant by 'cat family'. Remind learners about the fox and ask what family the fox belongs to.

Then ask learners to say a sentence about a cat using the information they have been talking about. Remind learners that they have to write three sentences and to remember capital letters and full stops.

2 In this activity learners look at pictures with labels and make a list of animals that belong to the cat family. Ask learners how to write words in a list before they do the activity.

Extension: Learners could add other animals to the cat and/or dog family.

Answers

2 lion, tiger, leopard

Workbook page 22

Reading

1 Here learners are expected to complete a word search to reinforce animal vocabulary.

Before they do the activity, show them how to do a word search. Explain to learners that the words can go across the page or down the page and demonstrate by running your finger along and then down. Tell them that when they find a word in the word search, they should cross out this word in the box at the top. The first word, 'lion', has been found. Point out how the letters are arranged down the page and where the 'circle' has been drawn. Ask what should be done next – cross the word 'lion' out in the box at the top. Demonstrate another word in the same way and then ask learners to complete the word search.

Support: Some learners could work in pairs. Model the procedure with them if necessary.

2 Then learners work alone and match the sentences to the pictures. They should pay attention to the singular and plural forms of the nouns.

Answers

2 There are two foxes; The cat is playing.

Student's Book page 29

Reading and writing

Read the rhyme with learners. Then give them the opportunity to read out loud alone. Talk about what is happening in the rhyme and ask learners to predict what the next verse might be. ('Four little ducks went swimming one day', and so on.)

1 Ask learners to read the rhyme again and find the answers to the questions. They then write the pairs of rhyming words in the rhyme. Learners could learn the rhyme and recite it to their peers.

Extension: Learners could write the second verse of the rhyme, modelling it on the first verse.

2 This activity involves recognising the common word ending *–s* when *s* is added to a word to make the plural form. Before turning to the activity, ask learners to find the word 'duck' and the word 'ducks' in the rhyme. Invite learners to say what makes the words different. (One is singular and the other is plural.)

Then write pairs of words on the whiteboard. For example: 'dog – dogs', 'cup – cups', 'bed – beds', 'bag – bags', 'ring – rings', 'song – songs', 'sack – sacks', 'lock – locks'.

At this stage, only use words where the plural is formed by adding *–s* to the root word.

Ask learners what they notice about the pairs of words and to explain why they are different. The first word in each pair is used to speak about one thing, for example one dog or one ring. The second word in each pair is used to talk about more than one thing, for example two beds, three locks or four cups.

Ask learners to write the plural form of words.

Suggested words: 'hat', 'cup', 'fan', 'tin', 'mug', 'bag', 'van', 'net', 'zip', 'tub', 'hens'.

Before learners do the activity, draw their attention to 'number' words. Ask learners to read the words, inviting them to say what strategy would be good to use if they are unsure of any or all of the words. Confirm that the pictures help. Discuss how phonics will not always help with some words, for example *one* is an exception word. Other exception words include 'said', 'come', 'he'. Many of the exception words are also included in the 'first 100 high-frequency words' (see page 7 of this resource).

Refer learners back to page 26 of the Student's Book and ask them to find any plural words (foxes, bins, berries, worms, spiders, mice and birds). Write them on the whiteboard. Elicit from learners that the words are all plural words but have different endings. Ask learners to say the words that add *–s* to make the plural form and highlight. Ask learners to say the three words that do not follow 'the add *–s'* rule (foxes, berries, mice). Tell learners that most words add *–s* to make the plural but there are also other ways of making plurals and they are going to look at one of the ways, adding *–es*

Ask learners to scan page 26 to find the word 'foxes' (there are seven instances of the word). Highlighter tape would be good for this activity.

Write some other words on the board that follow the pattern of adding *–es* to make the plural form and invite learners to read them.

Suggested words: boxes, brushes, glasses, dishes, watches, dresses, sandwiches, buses.

At a later date learners could play 'detective' and note any words, that add *–es* to make the plural form, when they are reading.

Hand out PCM 17: Plurals. Learners need to write the words on the signs in the shop window in two lists.

Answers to PCM 17

Plurals with *–s*: bats, flags, nets, hats, mugs.
Plurals with *–es*: glasses, boxes, buses, brushes, dishes.

The learners do activities 1 and 2.

Answers

1 five; day – away; quack – back
2 one duck; four frogs; three cats; five bats; two birds

Student's Book page 30

Reading and listening

This section involves reading and enjoying a poem about a lion. Look at the picture of the lion with the learners. Does the picture suggest anything about the lion?

Read the poem with learners and then talk about the words the author uses and why he chose them. Discuss what the words mean and how they make the reader feel about the lion. Is the picture a 'good match' for the words?

Learners then complete activities 2–4.

Answers

3 paws – jaws; quivers – shivers

5 In this activity learners have to write two sentences about an animal for a fact file. Before writing, ask learners to reread the fact file about foxes on page 26 and discuss the style of text and its features.

Bring the learners together and ask them to read aloud the sentences they have written.

Workbook page 23

Reading

In this activity, learners need to use what they have learned about ducks and lions. They make sentences about ducks and sentences about lions. Ask learners to do the activity.

Answers

Ducks have feathers. Ducks have beaks. Ducks are birds. Ducks have webbed feet. Lions live in the jungle. Lions roar. Lions belong to the cat family. Lions can run fast.

Thinking time

Discuss with learners which animals they prefer and why. Encourage learners to think about animals in the wild, animals in Safari parks, animals in zoos and animals as pets.

Weekly review

Use this rubric to assess learners' progress as they work through the activities this week. You can use the activities suggested beneath the table to follow up on your on-going assessment.

Level	Reading	Writing
■	Can confidently read labels and captions supported by illustrations in order to find information.	Understands the concept of writing information in a list and, with some support, can write lists for a purpose.
●	Can read labels and captions to find information.	Understands the concept of writing information in a list and can write lists for a purpose.
▲	Can read labels and captions to find information confidently.	Fully understands the concept of writing information in a list and can write lists for a purpose.

Support: Use your own headings or some of the suggestions in the Extension list below. Ask learners to say what they are going to write under a given heading. Learners should then write the list. You should act as scribe, if appropriate, to create lists with the learners.

Extension: Learners should write a list of their choice and give it an appropriate heading.

For example:

- colours
- food I like to eat
- games I like to play
- people in my family
- days of the week.

End of unit task

The Workbook activity on page 23 can be used together with PCM 18 as a reinforcement and consolidation task of the skills learned in this unit.

Unit 4 The moon

Unit overview

As learners work through this unit, they will read a story aloud and then retell and talk about the events in the story. *Bot on the Moon* is a simple fantasy story.

The unit could be part of a study about the sun, moon and stars.

Learners will have opportunities to read words with final and initial adjacent consonants by blending letters. They will also practise segmenting the words to spell them.

They will have opportunities to read and write high-frequency words and other familiar words.

Introducing the unit

The unit could be introduced by discussing and listing places (real or imaginary) where learners would most like to go. After eliciting some initial ideas from learners, steer the discussion to an imaginary trip to the moon. Tell them that they are going to visit the moon and discuss the following questions with them.

- How would you get there?
- What might you take with you?
- What might you see?
- What might you do?

If learners are interested in the topic, extend this discussion and spend some time finding out about the moon and the conditions on it.

Week 1

Key strands and substrands: Lesson outcomes

Reading

- Explore the cover and title of a simple fantasy story
- Read a story aloud in pairs
- Use phonic knowledge in reading and identifying unfamiliar words
- Answer questions about characters and events in a story
- Explore the differences in context and events between stories and real life
- Know the letters of the alphabet and recite them in order
- Find information by looking at pictures and reading labels
- Reread a text, showing understanding of capital letters and full stops in sentences
- Explore the use of 'and' in sentences

Writing

- Write a shopping list
- Record answers to simple questions

Speaking and listening

- Talk about a story clearly and audibly with a partner
- Listen to a story and think about questions
- Pause at full stops when reading aloud

Resources

- Student's Book pages 31–35
- Workbook pages 24–25
- Slideshow: *Bot on the Moon*
- Audio files: *Bot on the Moon; Mister Moon*
- PCM 19: Using 'and'

Workbook page 24

Reading and writing

In this section, learners are asked to complete a dot-to-dot picture of a rocket using the lower-case letters of the alphabet.

Revise alphabetical order by saying/singing alphabet rhymes with learners (see page 27 of this Teacher's Guide). It is useful to have an alphabet frieze displayed in the classroom for all learners to see. At this stage, some learners will need to be able to see the alphabet as well as hear it to aid learning.

Involve learners in a number of activities. For example:

- Say the name of a letter and ask a learner to find it on the alphabet frieze. Then ask: 'Is it near the beginning/near the end/in the middle of the alphabet?' Repeat for other letters.
- Recite the alphabet up to a certain letter, for example recite 'a, b, c, d,' and invite learners to join in with the rest. Repeat for other parts of the alphabet.
- Give learners opportunities to practise giving the name of the next (or previous) letter in the alphabet. For example:
  Say 'b' and invite a learner to say the name of the letter that comes next ('c').
  Say 'n' and invite a learner to say the name of the letter that comes next ('o').
  Say 'f' and invite a learner to say the name of the letter that comes before ('e').
  Repeat for other letters of the alphabet.

Learners need to know the difference between the name of a letter and the sound that it represents. Ensure that you use the correct term – name or sound – when speaking to learners. Give practice to help with this. For example:

- Say the sound of a letter and ask learners to say the name.
  The sound /s/ can be represented by 's' as in *sand* or 'c' as in *circus*. The sound /j/ can be represented by 'j' as in *jam* or 'g' as in *giant*.
- Say the name of a letter and ask learners to say the sound.
  The letter 'c' can represent the sound /c/ as in cat or /s/ as in cement. The letter 'g' can represent the sound /g/ as in *gate* or /j/ as in *gym*.

Student's Book pages 31–34

Reading and speaking

Ask learners to work with a partner and to look carefully at the cover of *Bot on the Moon* and then read the question below.

Invite learners to say what they think the story is going to be about and what might happen to the main character.

Student's Book page 35

Listening and speaking

Tell learners that you are going to read the story and while you read, they need to listen for two things. Ask learners to read the instructions and to say what they need to listen for.

Read the story. Check that learners found the answers to the questions through listening.

> *Answers*
> by rocket; a card and a moon rock

Reading and writing

1 Let learners read the story in pairs before asking individuals to read it aloud. Praise good use of reading strategies and fluency, encouraging pausing at full stops. Ask learners to read page 4 of the story silently before asking them to choose and read one sentence from the page aloud. How do they know it is a sentence?

Spend as much time as necessary on this section to ensure correct decoding of the text and to encourage reading with fluency. Encourage learners to use a variety of strategies, for example phonic skills, picture and context clues, reading on and rereading, to work out any unknown words.

Ask learners to read pages 5, 6 and 8 of the story again where the word 'and' appears. Discuss its use. For example, on page 5 'and' joins two things that Bot did. On page 6 'and' joins two things that Bot got at the shop. On page 8 'and' joins two things that Bot got out.

After reading, ask questions to check understanding.

- How did Bot go to the moon?
- What did Bot buy at the Moon Shop?
- Who did Bot send the postcard to?
- What did Bot lose?
- Did Bot get the club back?

2 Learners write answers to the questions. Encourage them to refer back to the text to check answers and spellings.

3 In this activity, learners need to write the sentences that are true. Remind learners that they have done an activity like this before (in Unit 1). Say a few sentences and ask learners to tell you if they are true or false. Bring learners together to check answers by asking them to find the part of the text that shows if their answer is correct. It is useful for them to start finding evidence for their answers. Highlighter tape could be useful here.

Answers

2 fast; a golf club

3 The moon had lots of hills; Bot had lost his club; The club hit Bot on his hat.

Speaking

Let the class identify events in the story that are similar or different to real life. Use the questions in the Student's Book to start this discussion. They should recognise that while people cannot really play golf on or send a postcard from the moon, people have travelled to the moon in a rocket. Encourage them to discuss other similarities and differences.

Workbook page 25

Reading and writing

1 Before learners do the activity, have a discussion about what Bot bought in the Moon Shop and what else he might have bought. Link to learners' own experiences of what they might buy as a souvenir when they visit a place of interest, for example a poster, a T-shirt, sweets or a toy.

Ask learners to look at the picture of the shop window and to tell you the name of an item in the window. Ask them if they can think of anything else that could be for sale in the Moon Shop, for example spare parts for rockets and clothes for travelling in a rocket.

2 Remind learners how a shopping list is written before they complete Bot's shopping list from items in the shop window.

Support: Work with individuals or groups to help them copy the names of the items accurately. Encourage the use of a 'marker' to keep the place of each word that learners copy. It can be difficult for some learners to move their eye from the word and then back to where they are writing without losing their place.

Extension:

1 Some learners might want to add items of their own to the shopping list.

2 Learners could draw or make items for a Moon Shop window display and then make labels for the items. Labels could be handwritten or typed.

Weekly review

Use this rubric to assess learners' progress as they work through the activities this week. You can use the activities suggested beneath the table to follow up on your on-going assessment.

Level	Reading	Writing
■	Reads familiar text well but needs support to tackle unfamiliar text.	Can write a shopping list choosing from a number of given items. Understands the use of 'and' in spoken language.
●	Reads well and is becoming more confident about using strategies to tackle unfamiliar words.	Can write a shopping list, choosing from a number of given items and then adding an item of their own. Understands the use of 'and' in spoken language and in text.
▲	Reads well and uses strategies independently to tackle unfamiliar words.	Can write a shopping list, choosing from a number of given items and then add items of their own. Uses 'and' appropriately in spoken language and recognises its use in text.

Support: Give learners PCM 19: Using 'and', and ask them to complete the phrases using 'and' and a visual clue.

Extension: Ask learners to say sentences with the word 'and' in them before asking them to write sentences. You should decide how many sentences the learners should write.

Week 2

Key strands and substrands: Lesson outcomes

Reading

- Understand words and sentences in a text, using phonic knowledge
- Blend sounds represented by adjacent consonants
- Understand when full stops and capital letters are used
- Explore rhyme in a story
- Identify sentences
- Use pictures to work out words
- Understand and use high frequency words

Writing

- Identify letters for adjacent consonants
- Relate rhyme to shared spelling patterns
- Write simple sentences using capital letters and full stops
- Spell familiar words accurately, including common exception words
- Write a postcard
- Sequence actions by ordering sentences

Resources

- Student's Book pages 36–38
- Workbook pages 26–28
- PCM 20: Phonics – adjacent consonants at the end of words
- PCM 21: Phonics – adjacent consonants at the beginning of words
- PCM 22 and 23: Phonics – adjacent consonants at the beginning of words
- PCM 24: Consonant-consonant-vowel-consonant words

Workbook page 26

Reading

This activity assesses learners' decoding of a familiar text and their understanding of the story. Learners match the beginning of sentences with their endings.

Answers

Bot zoomed past all the twinkling stars.
He sent the card to his mum.
Bot was back with Mum.
Bot was on a trip to the moon.
The club hit Bot on his hat.
Bot landed on the moon.

Student's Book page 36

Sounds and spelling

The activities in this section focus on reading words with final adjacent consonants and then writing words that rhyme with 'fast'.

1 Before learners do this activity, spend some time teaching them about adjacent consonants (consonant clusters) at the end of words. Tell them that there will be two sounds at the end of the words you are going to say and that they should listen carefully to hear both (*s* and *t* to make *st*).

Ask learners to identify the sounds at the end of the words 'fast', 'test', 'lost' and 'just'. Pronounce both consonants in the final consonant cluster carefully. (In everyday speech, one of these often becomes dominant.)

Ask learners to read the sentence in the box and find the word 'fast'.

2 Say the word 'nest' slowly and clearly and ask learners how many sounds they can hear (four sounds). Ask one learner to write the word 'nest' on the whiteboard.

Repeat the procedure for other words, for example: 'fast', 'test', 'rust', 'last', 'must', 'mast', 'jest', 'past', 'west', 'just', 'best', 'pest' and 'dust'. Ask learners to write some of the words to dictation, reminding them that each word has four letters.

Once you have done this, you could do the same for words ending in *–nt, –lt* and *–ft*. Remind learners to relate rhyme to shared spelling pattern, for example *fast*, *last*, *mast*, *past*.

Suggested words:

- 'went', 'tent', 'bent', 'sent', 'dent', 'lent', 'pant', 'mint', 'tint'
- 'melt', 'felt', 'belt', 'kilt', 'wilt', 'tilt'
- 'soft', 'loft', 'raft', 'gift', 'lift', 'left'.

Ask learners to complete activity 2.

Other consonant clusters that need to be taught using the same procedure are *lf, mp, nd, lk* and *sk*.

Suggested words:

- 'elf', 'self', 'shelf', 'golf'
- 'camp', 'damp', 'lamp', 'ramp', 'bump', 'dump', 'jump', 'hump', 'lump', 'limp'
- 'band', 'hand', 'land', 'sand', 'bend', 'lend', 'send', 'mend', 'pond', 'fond'
- 'milk', 'silk', 'bulk', 'hulk', 'sulk'
- 'ask', 'mask', 'task', 'risk', 'tusk', 'rusk', 'desk', 'tusk'.

These phrases can be used as dictation to check and assess spelling in this unit:

- Junk on a bunk.
- A mint on a desk.
- Dust on a lamp.
- A vest in a nest.
- A bump and a jump.
- A hand in the sand.
- A nest in the loft.
- A mask on a shelf.
- A gift in a lift.

Use PCM 20 either as a reinforcement activity or to assess skills in this area.

Answers

2 last; past; mast

Reading and writing

The focus of this section is the concept of a sentence – identifying sentences in a text and pausing at full stops when reading.

Give learners opportunities to highlight sentences in a familiar text. A good activity is to give learners a piece of copied text and highlighter pens. Then read a short sentence from the copied text for learners to find and highlight. Remind them to start highlighting at the beginning of the sentence (the capital letter) and to end at the full stop. They should then find and highlight another sentence using a different colour for each sentence.

Before learners do activities 1–4, ask them to read the questions aloud and check that they know exactly what is being asked.

Answers

2 three sentences

3 Bot; The; It

Workbook page 27

Sounds and spelling

Before learners do this activity, spend some time revising adjacent consonants (consonant clusters) at the end of words. Give them opportunities to identify adjacent final sounds in spoken words. Use some of the words from the guidance on teaching adjacent consonants (consonant clusters). Ask learners to write the two letters that represent the sounds they hear. Say the words clearly, with emphasis on the final adjacent consonants.

Ask learners to do the activity.

Answers

lk – milk; ft – raft; st – nest; nt – tent; nd – hand; lf – golf; lt – belt; nd – pond; st – vest

Student's Book page 37

Sounds and spelling

The focus of activity 1 is adjacent sounds at the beginning of words. Before learners do this activity, it may be necessary to spend some time teaching them about adjacent consonants (consonant clusters) at the beginning of words.

Tell learners that you are going to say words with two sounds at the beginning. They have to listen carefully to hear both sounds (*t* and *r*). Pronounce both consonants in the initial consonant cluster clearly. Say the word 'trip' slowly and ask learners to say how many sounds they can hear (four sounds). Ask a learner to write the word 'trip' on the whiteboard.

Repeat the procedure for other words: 'trap', 'trod', 'trim' and 'trot'. Ask learners to write the words to dictation, reminding them that each word has four letters.

There are a number of adjacent consonants where the second consonant is *r*, for example: *br, cr, dr, fr, gr* and *pr*. Write the clusters *br, cr, dr, fr, gr, pr* and *tr* on cards and stick the cards on the whiteboard. Tell learners that you will say a word and they need to say and point to the two letters that the word starts with.

Suggested words:

- 'bridge', 'brass', 'broom', 'brick', 'brush'
- 'crab', 'cry', 'crown', 'cross', 'crust'
- 'drawer', 'drip', 'dragon', 'drink', 'drum'
- 'friend', 'frog', 'frill', 'frock', 'fruit'
- 'grab', 'gran', 'grapes', 'grin', 'grass'
- 'pram', 'press', 'present', 'prize', 'pretty'
- 'train', 'truck', 'trailer', 'track', 'tractor'.

Say some of the words above and ask learners to write the first two letters they hear in each word. Learners should not be asked to write the whole word at this stage.

PCM 21 can be used at this stage to reinforce the concepts.

Use the same procedure to teach other consonant clusters at the beginning of words, for example, *bl, cl, fl, gl, pl, sk, sl, sm, sn, sp, st* and *sw*.

PCMs 22 and 23 can be used to reinforce and assess the spelling of words with these consonant clusters.

Support: It can be difficult for some learners to hear the differences between clusters. Individual speech problems can also cause difficulties. Support and give additional practice.

Dictation: Use these sentences for dictation in this unit.

- Gran has a long dress.
- Greg has a plan.
- Brad has a drum.
- The pram is on the grass.
- The frog can swim.
- The fish is in the pond.
- Mum went to the bus stop.
- Glen can jump and skip.
- The plug is in the sink.
- The flag is on the cliff.
- The crab is on the sand.
- The desk has a flat top.

1 Learners are asked to say and write words with consonant clusters at the beginning of each word.

2 Here learners read high-frequency words, including the exception word 'he', and use them to complete sentences. More than one word is missing from each sentence. Tell learners to read the whole sentence and decide which words are needed so that the sentence makes sense before they write. The word 'the' needs to be used twice.

Learners should have on-going practice in reading and writing high-frequency words and use the 'look, say, cover, write and check' method for learning to spell the words.

Answers

1 club; frog; flag; plug; drum

2 got; and; the; He; the; to; his

Reading and writing

1 Before learners do the activity, discuss what might be included in a picture postcard from the moon.

2 Before learners do activity 2, invite a learner to read the message on the postcard from Bot. Ask learners if they have ever received a postcard and invite them to tell the class who sent it to them and where it came from. Then, in pairs, ask learners to discuss what they might write on a postcard sent from the moon. Invite learners to say what they will write. After writing, invite some learners to read the messages they have written. Remind learners to speak clearly and audibly, and to show some awareness of their audience. Invite listeners to ask a question or comment positively about what they heard.

Workbook page 28

Reading and writing

This section involves completing sentences with words from *Bot on the Moon*. The words all have adjacent consonant sounds at the beginning of the word, at the end of the word, or both. There are no words for learners to copy, and while the purpose of the activity is to write the words from memory, it is important to ensure that learners know what words are missing. If necessary, allow them to work in pairs to read the sentences and work out the missing words together.

Support: Some learners may need to refer back to the text to find the correct word. Allow them to do this only after they have tried to work it out.

Answers

1 trip **2** Blast **3** fast **4** past **5** sent **6** trip

Student's Book page 38

Reading and writing

In this section, learners are asked to read sentences and then to write them in the correct order. They then write a sentence to say what Bot did next. Encourage learners to use the pictures and to look for clues in the text to work out the order before they start writing.

For example: Bot got out the moon rock and his best golf club.

Question: What tells the reader that this is the first sentence?

Answer: Bot had to get the moon rock and his best golf club out *before* he could hit the moon rock.

After learners have finished writing, remind them to read the sentences they have written and check that the order makes sense. Allow them to work in pairs to check and assess each other's work. Peer assessment is an important and valuable tool for learning.

Support: The sentences could be copied and given to learners. This way they can manipulate the text until they get the correct order before they write the sentences themselves.

Answers

2 Bot got out the moon rock and his best golf club.
He hit the moon rock.
It was a big hit.
Bot let go of the club.

Weekly review

Use this rubric to assess learners' progress as they work through the activities this week. You can use the activities suggested beneath the table to follow up on your on-going assessment.

Level	Reading	Writing
■	Can read words with consonant clusters at the beginning and at the end of words but needs regular practice to improve accuracy.	Can write words with consonant clusters when dictated as individual words.
●	Can read words with consonant clusters at the beginning and at the end of words with accuracy.	Can write words with consonant clusters when dictated as individual words and in written exercises.
▲	Can read words with consonant clusters at the beginning and at the end of words with speed and accuracy.	Can write words with consonant clusters when dictated as individual words, in written exercises and in their own writing. Spells them well in own writing most of the time.

Support: Create four 3 x 3 'bingo cards' with the following words on:

- Bingo board 1: sand, desk, drum, sink, crab, flat, flag, milk, plan
- Bingo board 2: grab, plan, swim, jump, flag, drip, pond, milk, drum
- Bingo board 3: drum, crab, flat, sand, desk, pond, sink, drip, sand
- Bingo board 4: crab, grab, drum, milk, desk, swim, jump, plan, flag

Hand out the bingo cards and counters to 2–4 learners.

Call words from this list: sand, desk, drum, sink, crab, flat, flag, milk, plan, grab, swim, jump, drip, pond, vest.

Learners should place a counter on the word called if it is on their board. The learner who covers all the called words correctly is the winner.

Extension: Ask learners to complete PCM 24, where they are asked to read CCVC/CVCC words and match each word to its meaning. Encourage learners to read all words and all meanings before starting matching.

Week 3

Key strands and substrands: Lesson outcomes

Reading

- Retell a story verbally
- Understand the structure and sequence of events in a story
- Hear and read a simple poem and identify the rhyming words
- Express preferences about text choices

Writing

- Write a sentence using a capital letter and full stop
- Draw sequenced pictures to retell a story

Speaking and listening

- Listen to a poem
- Make a simple personal statement
- Work in pairs, taking turns reading
- Talk about own activities, expressing preferences

Resources

- Student's Book pages 39–40
- Workbook page 29
- Slideshow: *Mister Moon*
- Audio file: *Mister Moon*
- PCM 25: End of unit task

Student's Book page 39

Speaking, reading and writing

1 Working in pairs, learners retell the story to each other. Monitor that they are taking turns to speak and listen and that they are telling the events of the story in the correct sequence.

Support: It may be necessary to support some learners by asking questions such as, 'What happened after that? What happened next?' and so on.

2 This activity asks learners to draw a story map to illustrate the story from 'Blast off!' to the point when Bot got a card at the Moon Shop. Discuss the main events in the sequence:

- The rocket went fast.
- It zoomed past the stars.
- It landed on the moon.
- Bot went up and down the hill.
- He got a card and a moon rock at the Moon Shop.

Tell learners that there should be five pictures, one for each part of the story on their story map. If further scaffolding for this task is necessary, provide learners with a five-frame story map template. Examples of the first and last pictures in the sequence have been shown for the learners. Talk with them about where their first picture should be positioned on the page and in what direction the pictures should go.

Extension: Ask learners to write a sentence under one or more pictures. You will need to decide what is appropriate for individual learners.

3 Learners are asked to draw a robot and give it a name before writing a sentence about their robot. Remind learners about a capital letter at the beginning and a full stop at the end of the sentence.

Student's Book page 40

Listening, reading and writing

Mister Moon is a poem for learners to listen to, read and enjoy.

1 Read the poem to learners and then read it again while they follow and join in with the words.

Take some time to discuss the poem and talk about how it is written. It is written in rhyming couplets, which are two lines of poetry of about the same length that rhyme. Rhyming words are words that sound the same when spoken but they do not necessarily have to be spelled the same.

Examples of rhyming couplets:

It's hard to see the butterfly
Because he flies across the sky.

Lightning, thunder all around,
Soon the rain falls on the ground.

2 Give learners time to read the poem in pairs. Ask learners, in turn, to read aloud one of the rhyming couplets from the poem and to identify the rhyming words in the couplet that they read. They then write the rhyming words in pairs.

Learners should memorise the poem and recite it to their peers.

Support: Some learners may learn one or two couplets from the poem.

Answers

sky – eye; go – hello; see – me; bright – night

Workbook page 29

Reading and writing

This section follows on from Student's Book page 40. Here learners complete each rhyming couplet by choosing the correct ending from those provided. Ask learners to read the poem again, and then check that they can read the poem endings before they do the activity.

Answers

with his big bright eye.; Mister Moon! Hello!; to follow me?; Mister Moon! Good night!

Thinking time

At the end of the unit, discuss with learners which type of fiction they prefer and why – the fantasy story *Bot on the Moon* or the poem *Mister Moon* written in rhyming couplets. Support learners to make a simple statement about why they preferred one to the other. Books should be available for learners to read and enjoy similar stories and poems.

Weekly review

Use this rubric to assess learners' progress as they work through the activities this week. You can use the activities suggested beneath the table to follow up on your on-going assessment.

Level	Listening and speaking
■	Can retell the events of a story but needs some support to sequence them.
●	Can retell a story with the events in sequence.
▲	Speaks clearly and can retell a story with the events in sequence.

Support: Highlight illustrations that show the main events of a familiar story to support learners with the activity below.

Extension: Reread a familiar story before asking learners to work in groups of three to discuss the main ideas of the story. Each learner should have responsibility for one part of the story – first, next, last of all.

End of unit task

Hand out PCM 25 and ask learners to complete it to make sure they are able to deal with consonant clusters at the beginning and end of words. Before starting, ensure that learners know what the pictures represent, for example a mask on a shelf.

Unit 5 *Funny Fish*

Unit overview

As learners work through this unit, they will read a story aloud and then retell and talk about the events in the story. *Funny Fish* is a story with patterned and predicable language. *A Fine Feathered Fish* is a nonsense rhyme.

The unit could be part of a study about how fish and sea animals protect themselves or the wider topic of camouflage in animals.

Learners will have the opportunity to develop an understanding of a group of letters that make one sound: *–igh.*

They will also have opportunities to read and write high-frequency words and other familiar words.

Introducing the unit

Introduce the unit by telling learners that they are going to read a book about fish. Explain that they are not fish that behave the way we think they do; they are fish that can talk. Ask individual learners to tell the class about any films or programmes they have seen in which fish can talk. There are many such films and learners may have seen *Finding Nemo*, *Shark Tale* or *Help! I'm a Fish*.

Week 1

Key strands and substrands: Lesson outcomes

Reading

- Explore the title page of a book and make inferences from it
- Respond verbally to questions about a story
- Read a simple story and make predictions
- Use phonic knowledge to read decodable words and to sound out some elements of unfamiliar words
- Explore the rhythm of a text
- Show understanding of a story, including explicit meaning
- Identify and describe characters in a story
- Explore nouns and verbs ending in *–ing*, and recognise common words

Writing

- Record answers to questions in a list
- Write a simple non-fiction sentence using a capital letter and a full stop, including relevant information
- Spell familiar words accurately
- Use simple organisational features appropriate to the text type (labels)

Speaking and listening

- Have a pair discussion, taking turns to speak, listening and understanding opinions and providing relevant information
- Reread sentences aloud with fluency and expression

Resources

- Student's Book pages 41–46
- Workbook page 30
- Slideshow: *Funny Fish*
- Audio file*: Funny Fish*
- PCM 26: Spelling common words
- PCM 27: Phonics skills and context

Student's Book pages 41–42

Reading and speaking

1 Read the instructions with learners. Then ask them to read the first part of the instructions with you. Ask:

- How many words are in this sentence?
- What is the last word in the sentence?
- What comes after the last word in the sentence?
- What word does the next sentence start with?
- What word does the next sentence end with?
- How many sentences are in the instructions?
- What do you notice about 'Look' and 'book'?

Give learners time to read what they are being asked to talk about, in pairs and individually, before inviting a learner to read aloud. Model correct reading and ensure that learners understand what is being asked of them before they do the activity. Monitor learners, ensuring that they talk about what has been asked, that they take turns to speak, and that they listen carefully when their partner speaks, including when their partner is saying what they think.

Then bring the class together for a discussion and check the points that they have discussed.

Move on to talk about the fact that the page is a title page. Ask:

- How does it differ from the cover of a book?

Talk briefly about how an author writes a book (the words of the book), and an illustrator draws the pictures.

2 Read page 42 with learners, emphasising the rhythm. Encourage them to join in using the pattern of the text to support decoding. Ask learners to find rhyming words in the text, noting where they are positioned.

Ask learners to look at the word 'swimming' – what do they notice at the beginning of the word? (the consonant cluster *sw*) Explain to learners that recognising *sw*, along with the context of the story, helps them to know what the word is. Draw their attention to the end of the word and ask what they notice. (It ends in *–ing*.)

Talk about what the fish are doing. (swimming) Swimming is an action word. Ask learners if they can think of any other action words, for example 'walking', 'running', 'lifting'. Tell learners that action words are called verbs.

Ask learners to predict what happens next in the story.

Student's Book pages 42–45

Reading and writing

1 Ask learners to use the picture to predict which fish said, "Look at me!" Bring the class together to discuss what they have been talking about and to check understanding. Talk about the expressions on the faces of the fish and what those expressions tell the reader.

2 Read the rest of the story with learners, emphasising the rhythm, and encourage learners to join in using the pattern of the text to support decoding. Ask individuals to read parts of the story aloud. Monitor for fluency and expression.

Spend as much time as necessary on this activity to ensure correct decoding of the text and to allow practice in fluent reading. Encourage learners to use a variety of strategies – phonic skills, picture and context clues, reading on and rereading – to work out any unknown words.

Ask learners to look at page 43 and to find another word starting with *sw* – 'swish'. Talk about why 'swish' is written three times and why there are three dots after the last 'swish'.

Ask learners to look at the word 'bright' on page 42 and model how to read it. Use phonic knowledge to tackle *br,* and how the word ends with a *'t'* and help learners to see how the context and the grammar of the sentence help to predict the word. There is a 'tricky' bit, the letters *'igh'* in the middle. These three letters make the long sound /i/. You will look more closely at the word 'bright' and its spelling pattern with learners in Week 2.

Ask some questions to ensure understanding. For example:

- How many fish were swimming in the sea?
- Which fish was eaten first by the shark?
- What colour was the second fish to be eaten?
- Why wasn't the third fish eaten?

Reading the story provides an ideal opportunity for learners to read high-frequency words (*in, was, fish, three, red, he, like, sea, said*) in context and then to learn to spell them. This is something that can be done throughout the three weeks that it takes to cover this unit. Use the 'look, say, cover, write and check' method as one of your strategies. Some of these words are also exception words.

Learners need to get into the habit of looking at words with intent: observing details, highlighting difficult parts, visualising and committing a word to memory. Learners with poor visual memories may need extra support and practice to commit words to memory successfully.

Learners can work in pairs and then individually to read the rest of the story again. Spend as much time as necessary on this section to ensure accurate decoding and to encourage reading with fluency.

Support: Support individuals and small groups when necessary while they are reading.

3 Learners are asked to say if sentences are true or false. Ask them to find evidence in the text for their answers. For example:

The fish were swimming in a pond.

False: The evidence for this is on page 1. The fish were swimming in the sea.

This is a good strategy for learners to begin to develop at this early stage, and you should check as you monitor that learners are using it.

Answers

3 One fish was red; The big fish ate two fish; One fish was yellow like the sun.

Workbook page 30

Reading

This activity assesses learners' decoding of the now familiar text and their understanding of the story. They match the beginning of sentences with their endings.

Answers

Three funny fish were swimming in the sea; I am bright and funny and red; That was the end of the funny red fish; I am yellow – as bright as the sun!; I can look like a stone; The big bad fish leaves me alone!

Student's Book page 46

Reading and writing

Before learners do the activities in this section, have a discussion with them about the fish. Talk about words to describe the different fish, eliciting the words in activity 1: 'red', 'clever', 'brown', 'bossy', 'shy', 'bright', 'funny', 'boastful' and 'spotty'.

'Fish' is a noun. A noun can be:

- a person, girl, boy, Ann, Ajay
- a place, home, school, country
- a thing, table, bus, cat, fish.

Ask learners to describe why the funny brown fish was saved from the shark. Introduce the word 'camouflage'. What other creatures use camouflage to hide in the wild? Use images of animals using camouflage. Ask why the red and yellow fish were eaten. Was it only because they were brightly coloured?

Read through activities 1–5 with learners, checking that they know what to do.

Show on the whiteboard how to set out the two lists for activity 2.

Ask learners where they will find the words to complete the sentences in activity 3. Draw their attention to the word 'and' in the text.

For activity 4, talk with learners about what labels they should write on their pictures of fish and where to write them.

For activity 5, remind learners what you will be looking for in their written sentences.

Answers

2 red fish: red, bossy, bright, funny, boastful
brown fish: clever, brown, shy, spotty

3 Answers can include any two of the following: clever, brown, shy, spotty. Answers can include any two of the following: red, bossy, bright, funny, boastful.

Weekly review

Use this rubric to assess learners' progress as they work through the activities this week. You can use the activities suggested beneath the table to follow up on your on-going assessment.

Level	Reading	Writing
■	Becoming more accurate with decoding and has a good understanding of what they read.	Can draw and label a drawing.
●	Reads with increasing accuracy and has a good understanding of what they read.	Can draw and label a drawing accurately.
▲	Reads with increasing fluency and accuracy, and has a very good understanding of what they read.	Can draw and label a detailed drawing accurately.

Support: Give learners PCM 26 and ask them to complete the sentences by choosing one of the words in the box by each sentence.

Extension: Give learners the cloze procedure PCM 27, which is a more challenging version of PCM 26 in which they work out words from context and write them with a model.

Week 2

Key strands and substrands: Lesson outcomes

Reading

- Use pictures to support understanding of words
- Use phonic knowledge to read decodable words and to sound out unfamiliar words
- Begin to recognise colour words
- Explore sentences that contain 'and'
- Identify the sound represented by the letters 'igh'
- Understand words and sentences encountered in texts
- Know which letters are vowels and the most common sounds associated with them

Writing

- Spell familiar words accurately
- Relate rhyme to shared spelling patterns
- Write descriptive sentences using capital letters and full stops

Resources

- Student's Book pages 47–48
- Workbook pages 31–33

Workbook page 31

Writing

Before learners do the activity, talk about the pictures and invite learners to say what they might write about. Encourage them to speak clearly, making what they say as interesting as possible. Then choose one learner's description of what is happening in the picture and model how to write it. Give a running commentary as you write, for example: 'I am starting with a capital letter because we always start sentences with a capital letter. I remember how to write "fish" by sounding it out: *f-i-sh*. At the end of the word "fish" there are two letters that make one sound.' Continue to voice where appropriate as you write. If necessary, ask another learner for their description and repeat the process.

Support: Work with a small group and invite each learner to say what they are going to write. Support them as they write. Scribe for individual learners if necessary. Learners could then write below your text.

Student's Book page 47

Reading and writing

This section focuses on reading and spelling common words. Tell learners that the words are all colour words and this should help them to read the words. Ask: 'How?' Then say: '"Blue", "black" and "brown" all start with *b* so how do we know which is which? We need to look at the next letter. *Br* helps with "brown" but "blue" and "black" both have *bl* at the beginning. What else? "Black" has a /c/ sound at the end and "brown" has an /n/ sound at the end.'

Remind learners that if they use two colour words in a sentence, they need to use 'and'.

Give learners opportunities to practise writing the colour words. They should look at a word and highlight any part of that word that they find tricky. Think of what would help them to remember how to spell the word and get them to practise writing it.

Ask learners to do the activities.

Answers

3 The flower is yellow and red. / The flower is red and yellow.
The owl is brown and black. / The owl is black and brown.
The bird is blue and green. / The bird is green and blue.
The butterfly is purple and white. / The butterfly is white and purple.

Workbook page 32

Reading and spelling

This section focuses on finding high-frequency words in the story and using them to complete sentences.

Some learners may be able to scan the text to see if the words appear on the pages. A useful strategy is to place a 'marker' underneath the first line of print and pull it down as they read each line of print. Other learners will need to focus on more detailed reading. Again a 'marker' would be beneficial.

Remind learners that when they are looking for certain words in the story, they do not need to read every word.

Learners do activities 1 and 2.

Answers

1 *said*: pages 2, 4, 8, 10, 12
came: pages 5, 9, 11
were: pages 1, 7
Then: pages 5, 9, 11
was: pages 6, 10,

2 came; said; were; was; Then

Student's Book page 48

Sounds and spelling

This section focuses on the word 'bright' in the text and uses rhyme to relate it to the spelling pattern *ight*. *Bright* is a word with the trigraph *igh* in the middle. A trigraph is a group of three letters making one sound.

Before learners do the activities, use the word 'bright' as a starting word, as it is one they have read in the story. Ask learners what sounds they hear: *b-r-igh-t*. There are four sounds in the word 'bright'.

Ask learners to look at the word 'bright' in their books. Remind them that sometimes, more than one letter makes one sound. Ask them if they can work out which letters make the long *i* sound. Confirm that the letters are *igh*. Write the word 'bright' on the whiteboard with learners' help by asking which letter comes first, second, and so on.

Now use onset and rhyme to write other words ending in *–ight*. Point to the word 'bright' on the whiteboard and ask learners what word they would get if they changed *br* for *fr* and then for *fl*. Draw their attention to the consonant clusters at the beginning of these words.

Repeat the procedure with the words 'fight', 'light', 'might', 'night', 'right' and 'sight'.

Tell learners that this is only one way to write the long *i* sound and that they will learn about others at another time.

1 Ask learners to practise writing the group of letters *igh* for speed and accuracy. They then do activity 1.

2 Learners use some of the *ight* words to complete and then copy sentences.

There are other trigraphs, for example *tch* as in *watch*, *air* as in *chair*, and *dge* as in *hedge* – which should be identified in texts as they arise.

Dictation: Here are some sentences that are suitable for dictation in this unit.

- I might go to the shops.
- I went to bed last night.
- The sun is bright.
- I cut my right hand.
- The big light is on.

Answers

1 fright; light; fight; night; sight; might; right; tight; flight

2 light; night; bright; right

Workbook page 33

Sounds and spelling

This section focuses on words with adjacent consonants and the vowels of the words. Learners change the vowel sound to make new words.

Ask learners to say, 'Angry elephants in orange underwear' to remind them of the vowels – *a, e, i, o* and *u*.

Ask learners to say the names of the vowels and then the sounds of the vowels in sequence. A good aid is to spread the fingers of one hand and point to each finger in turn as you say the words 'Angry elephants in orange underwear' or *a, e, i, o, u* (names and sounds).

Give learners practice in changing the vowel sounds in words to make new words. Write a word like 'lift' on the whiteboard. Say: 'Change the vowel to *e*. What word will it be?' ('left')

Repeat the procedure with 'fast' ('fist'), 'must' ('mist'/'mast'), 'land' ('lend'), 'limp' ('lamp'/'lump') and 'sink' ('sank'). For this activity, learners could use whiteboards to write the words, or magnetic letters.

Learners then do the activity in the Workbook.

Answers

rust; lump; send; pest; last; damp; band; loft

Weekly review

Use this rubric to assess learners' progress as they work through the activities this week. You can use the activities suggested beneath the table to follow up on your on-going assessment.

Level	Reading	Writing
■	Can read words with the long vowel *i* represented by *igh* when the words are in rhyming lists.	Can write simple sentences with a capital letter and a full stop. Often needs a model to spell familiar common words.
●	Can read words with the long vowel *i* represented by *igh* with accuracy. Recognises and reads them when the *igh* word is embedded in text.	Can write simple sentences with a capital letter and a full stop. Can spell some familiar common words accurately.
▲	Can read words with the long vowel *i* represented by *igh* with speed and accuracy. Recognises and reads them when the *igh* word is embedded in text.	Can write simple sentences with a capital letter and a full stop. Can spell familiar common words accurately.

Support: Learners should be given further practise in writing familiar common words. 'Look, say, cover, write and check' is a useful strategy to use:

- When learners look at a word that they have difficulty with, they must be encouraged to look at it with intent and ask themselves "What is the tricky part of this word for me?"
- For example: 'was'. When a learner looks at this word, they might say "I have to remember the vowel sound in the middle is written with the letter 'a' and not an 'o'."
- When learners cover the word, encourage them to visualise it before writing.
- When learners write the word, encourage them to say aloud the names of the letters as they write.

Extension: Ask learners to identify words in a text that they are unsure about spelling. They should use the 'look, say, cover, write and check' strategy to secure their spelling.

Week 3

Key strands and substrands: Lesson outcomes

Reading

- Read a poem independently and in pairs
- Show understanding of words and sentences in a poem and use pictures as cues to understanding
- Explore sounds and words, and understand rhyme in a poem
- Recite the alphabet in order
- Use phonic knowledge to read decodable words and to sound out some elements of unfamiliar words
- Respond verbally to simple questions about texts
- Begin to make choices about books to read or listen to for pleasure

Writing

- Begin to write a simple poem using the structure of a familiar poem
- Copy a poem neatly, forming upper- and lower-case letters correctly

Speaking and listening

- Recite a simple poem, showing awareness of rhythm and pausing at full stops
- Talk about own activities, expressing preferences
- Speak audibly and clearly with familiar people
- Talk in pairs, speaking clearly, taking turns and showing awareness of each other as audience
- Listen and respond appropriately

Resources

- Student's Book pages 49–50
- Workbook pages 34–35
- Slideshows: *A Fine Feathered Fish; One, two, three, four, five; Going fishing; Nut Tree*
- Audio files: *A fine feathered fish; One, two, three, four, five; Going fishing; Nut Tree*
- PCM 28: End of unit task

Student's Book page 49

Reading and speaking

A Fine Feathered Fish is a nonsense rhyme for learners to read and enjoy.

Read the rhymes to learners with expression before asking them to join in reading. Take some time to discuss the poems, their content, the alliterative language and their rhyming patterns. Ask some questions, for example:

- How many fins did the furry fish have?
- What happened to the fine feathered fish?
- Why do you think the fine feathered fish yelled to the fish in the tins?
- Why did the person let the fish go in the second poem?
- What do you notice about some of the words/lines in the poem? (Some words rhyme; some words start with the same letter; two lines are the same.)

Learners should memorise the rhymes and, when ready, recite them to their peers showing an awareness of the rhythm of the poem.

Workbook page 34

Reading and writing

Learners complete the poem by selecting the correct endings for lines. Encourage learners to read the poem again after they have completed the activity to check that it reads correctly.

Answers

five furry fins; four fishy tins.; five furry fins; out of those tins!

Student's Book page 50

Reading and writing

1 In this activity, learners choose the correct words to complete sentences about the poem.

2–3 Before learners do activities 2 and 3, give them the opportunity to listen to and read some rhyming poems. Encourage learners to join in with some words and phrases, and pause with you at full stops.

You could read this traditional rhyme:

Going fishing

I took my shiny fishing rod
And went down to the sea.
There I caught a little fish
Which made…
One fish and me.

I took my shiny fishing rod
And went down to the sea.
There I caught a little crab
Which made…
One fish, one crab and me.

I took my shiny fishing rod
And went down to the sea.
There I caught a little clam
Which made…
One fish, one crab, one clam and me.

You could also use *Nut Tree* by Julia Donaldson, showing learners the text.

Nut Tree
by Julia Donaldson

Small, brown, hard, round,
The nut is lying underground.
Now a shoot begins to show,
Now the shoot begins to grow.
Tall, taller, tall as can be,
The shoot is growing into a tree.
And branches grow and stretch and spread
With twigs and leaves above your head.
And on a windy day
The nut tree bends, the branches sway.
The leaves fly off and whirl around,
And nuts go tumbling to the ground.
Small, brown, hard and round.

Once you have read and talked about some poems, encourage learners to contribute ideas to develop a class poem on the whiteboard. Then ask learners to write their own poems using a writing frame such as this one:

My friend the alien has seven blue toes,
My friend the alien has ____________ *nose.*

Here learners need to include adjectives, not rhyming words.

Move on to frameworks where the learner completes the line with a rhyming word. For example:

My friend the alien has seven blue toes,
My friend the alien ________________.

It may be necessary to ask learners to generate a list of words that rhyme with 'toes' to help them before they do this.

Ask learners to do activities 2 and 3.

Answers

1 dish; furry; four; my

Thinking time

Discuss with learners which fish they would prefer to be and why. Encourage learners to think about two of the fish being boastful and the other being shy. Was being boastful the best way to be? Remind learners about speaking audibly and clearly.

Workbook page 35

The alphabet

Have learners recite the alphabet. Then ask them to complete a dot-to-dot in the shape of a fish using capital letters.

Before learners do this activity, ask them to practice writing the alphabet. Then give learners practice writing the capital letter that corresponds to a given lower-case letter. You could write the lower-case letters on the whiteboard or hold up lower-case alphabet cards.

Weekly review

Use this rubric to assess learners' progress as they work through the activities this week. You can use the activities suggested beneath the table to follow up on your on-going assessment.

Level	Reading	Writing
■	Knows the names of most letters in the English alphabet and the most common sound associated with them. Can say or sing alphabet songs.	Can learn and recite a verse of poetry. The alliterative language made fluency difficult in *A Fine Feathered Fish*.
●	Knows the names of all the letters in the English alphabet and can associate most alphabet names and sounds. Can recite the alphabet in sequence.	Can learn and recite poetry using some expression.
▲	Knows the names of all the letters in the English alphabet and the most common sound associated with them. Can recite the alphabet.	Can learn and recite poetry, speaking clearly and with expression.

Support: Ensure that learners have daily practise with alphabet songs, rhymes and activities suggested in Units 1 and 2 to secure alphabet/sound relationship.

Extension: *Nut Tree* is a poem by Julia Donaldson. Donaldson has written many stories and poems in rhyme. Encourage learners join in with some words and phrases as you read the stories and poems to them. They could then choose a favourite to read with a partner or by themselves. For example:

- *Room on the Broom*, *A Squash and a Squeeze, Chocolate Mousse for a Greedy Goose.* All (and many more) by Julia Donaldson
- *Giraffes Can't Dance* by Giles Andreae
- *Duck in the Truck* by Jez Alborough
- *Green Eggs and Ham* by Dr Seuss.

End of unit task

PCM 28 can be used to assess learners' ability to work with rhyming words. Hand a copy of the PCM to each learner and ask them to complete it independently. Learners can choose which four pairs of rhyming words, from the poem, to write. Collect their work, check it and record the results on a record sheet.

Unit 6 Food

Unit overview

The focus is on non-fiction texts about types of food. Learners will have the opportunity to read information about food types supported by illustrations and they will be expected to find information from illustrations, text, labels, captions and signs.

Most school curricula deal with the topic of food and healthy eating in some way. This unit will supplement any work done on this topic in health or science lessons.

This topic also allows learners to discuss and explore cultural, religious and regional aspects of food and eating. It is valuable for learners to learn that different communities eat different types of food, depending on where they live, what is available locally and what beliefs and traditions they subscribe to.

Introducing the unit

The unit could be introduced by asking learners to talk about their favourite foods. Discuss different meal times, at what time of day different meals are eaten and what types of food are eaten at different meals. During the discussion, bring the conversation round to the different types of food that learners eat and so to the different food groups.

If possible, make a range of information about food available to the class. This can be in the form of books, articles, short videos or information from the internet. Draw up a table like this one:

Foods from plants	Foods from animals	Healthy foods	Unhealthy foods

Give learners some time to engage with the information available and then ask them to provide information to complete the table under each heading.

Week 1

Key strands and substrands: Lesson outcomes

Reading
- Read non-fiction texts and begin to understand that they have different purposes
- Use images and graphics to aid understanding of texts
- Find explicit information, including by reading labels
- Begin to show understanding of words and sentences in texts
- Use phonic knowledge to help read unfamiliar words
- Respond verbally to simple questions about texts read

Writing
- Write simple sentences using relevant vocabulary
- Begin to write for a purpose, creating labelled drawings
- Record answers to simple questions about texts

Speaking and listening
- Talk in pairs, speaking clearly, taking turns and showing awareness of each other as audience
- Make a simple personal statement
- Use some relevant vocabulary

Resources
- Student's Book pages 51–53
- Workbook pages 36–37
- Slideshows: *A healthy diet; Fish and seafood*
- Audio files: *A healthy diet; Fish and seafood*

Student's Book page 51

Listening and speaking

Read the title of the unit with learners and then ask them to look at the poster on page 51. Ask learners what they think the poster shows and where they might see a poster like this. Read the labels for each section of the poster with learners and ask them to point to each section in turn. Then ask questions, for example:

- Which foods should we eat most of? How can you tell from looking at the poster?
- Which food should we not each too much of? How can you tell from looking at the poster?

Ask learners to work in pairs. Give them time to look at the poster, talk about the food groups and what foods belong to each group. They should use the pictures and think of some other foods and where they belong.

Draw the class together and establish what the five food groups are. Write them on the whiteboard as headings and invite learners to name a food and to say which heading it should go under. Act as scribe.

Support: Help learners to read the text starting: 'Food gives…' by asking questions. For example:

- What do you think it is going to be about?
- Are there any words that you know?

If necessary, ask learners to find specific words, for example 'food', 'energy' and 'five'. When they have found 'five', ask: 'What do you think the word after "five" is?' Here learners should use the *gr* consonant cluster at the beginning of the word and the context of what they have been talking about to work out 'groups'.

Writing

Before learners turn to this section, spend some time talking about why we need food.

Learners need to use information from the text in the previous section to complete two sentences. They could then copy the first sentences on to paper and draw a picture of themselves doing something that needs energy. Under the picture they could write a caption, for example, 'I need energy to dance/play football/run/jump.' This could be displayed with a heading such as 'Food gives us energy'.

Answer

energy; each of the five food groups

Workbook page 36

Reading and writing

Recap the five food groups and invite learners to give one or two suggestions of foods that belong to each group. Write some of these on the whiteboard; they will help learners when they need to write themselves. The words should be displayed to support future writing. You should continue to display words like these as you work through the unit.

Point out the headings and ask learners to read them. Encourage learners to use initial sounds/clusters to help. Highlight the clusters *br* and *fr*; highlight *sh* where two letters make one sound; and highlight 'eggs' which has the common word ending *–s*. Learners should also note the word 'and' in each heading. Then invite them to say which food group is missing from the activity (sugar and fats).

Support: If learners need help, scribe the foods they say for the different food groups.

Student's Book page 52

Reading

Tell learners that they are going to find out more about one of the food groups – fish and seafood.

Ask learners to work in pairs. They should look at the pictures and try to identify what they can see. Then bring learners together and discuss the first two pictures. Ask questions like:

- What are the pictures of?
- Who uses fishing nets/rods?
- Where do people catch fish?

Try to elicit answers that will highlight vocabulary that is introduced in the text. Then ask learners to work in pairs and read the first paragraph about fish. Remind them to think about what they have been talking about as they read.

Read the paragraph together as a class before inviting individuals to read aloud. Then give learners time to read the rest of the text.

Remind learners again of the importance of looking at the pictures as they read – the pictures give information about what the text is about and, along with phonics and context clues, can help with reading some unfamiliar words. Follow up by asking learners what information they have learned about fish and seafood. Then ask:

- Is a lobster a fish or a sea creature?

- Is a tuna a fish or a sea creature?
- Which is the odd one out – prawn, lobster, eel or oyster? Why?

Ask learners which part of the text has information about seafood, where fish live, different kinds of fish and about fishing. It is important that learners begin to understand the importance of interacting with the text. Spend as much time as necessary on reading and understanding the text.

Student's Book page 53

Reading and writing

In this section, learners complete sentences about fish. Remind them to use the text on page 52 to find and check answers.

Point out that longer sentences often use linking words to join words and ideas. Ask them what linking words they can see in the questions here (they should identify the word 'and'). Talk about other simple connectives with learners if appropriate.

Answers

water; rivers, lakes, the sea; fishing rods, nets

Listening and speaking

Ask learners to work in pairs and look at the seafood in the pictures. Can they read the seafood words? Can they describe the different types shown? Then look at the words learners are not sure about and encourage them to use clues to work them out. For example, 'octopus' and 'oyster' both start with *o*. Can any other sounds in the words help? What sound is at the end of each word?

Invite learners to choose one of the sea creatures to describe to the class. Remind learners to speak audibly and clearly and to include relevant information.

Writing

Following on from the previous activity, learners are asked to draw three types of seafood and label them. Remind them to write the labels close to the pictures.

Listening and speaking

In this activity, learners work in pairs to answer two questions. Learners should think about the following when talking:

- Do you like eating fish and seafood?
- When do you eat it?
- How is it cooked?

Learners could then give a short presentation about fish and seafood to their peers. Give them time to prepare using resources available, such as non-fiction books, posters and the internet to help with this. Remind learners to include some relevant information. Monitor how clearly they speak and if they show some awareness of their audience.

Workbook page 37

Reading and writing

In this activity, learners choose the correct word to match a picture of fish or seafood. They then write the words.

Monitor the activity and assess how well learners can use initial sounds as a first strategy to read the words if they are not immediately known.

Extension: Ask learners to make an underwater scene. Show them a picture of tropical fish and discuss the colours and shapes of the fish. Learners then paint or draw pictures of brightly coloured fish on paper and cut them out. To make the underwater scene, they stick their pictures on a large sheet of paper. They can refer to Student's Book pages 42–44 in Unit 5: *Funny Fish* before they do this.

Answers

crab; eel; octopus; shrimp; squid; tuna; lobster; mussels

Weekly review

Use this rubric to assess learners' progress as they work through the activities this week. You can use the activities suggested beneath the table to follow up on your on-going assessment.

Level	Reading	Writing
■	Can use initial sounds as an initial strategy to read some interest words but then needs some support.	Can make a short presentation to peers but needs some prompts to keep to the topic being discussed.
●	Uses initial sounds as a first strategy and then, using the context of the word, is able to read most interest words.	Can make a short presentation to peers.
▲	Uses initial sounds as a first strategy and then, using the context of the word, is able to read most interest words.	Can confidently make a short presentation to peers.

Support: Give learners an opportunity to speak about something of personal interest to them – somewhere they have been or something they have done. They should tell three things about the subject they are going to talk about. For example: 'Yesterday I went to the museum with Grandma and Grandpa. My favourite thing was the Tyrannosaurus Rex. He is sometimes called T. Rex for short.' This could be an activity prepared at home.

Extension: Allow learners to talk about something of interest to them as above, but encourage them to use a visual aid to enhance their presentation. Discuss examples with learners. For example, a recipe would be good to show/talk about if they had been baking at home. Encourage them not just to show the book, but to explain how to use it. For example: 'I was making muffins with dad at the weekend. This is the recipe book we used. It's called… First we had to look at the contents to find what page the recipe was on. We turned to the page and found what ingredients we needed and how to make the muffins.'

Week 2

Key strands and substrands: Lesson outcomes

Reading

- Read and understand an information text that includes pictures
- Answer questions about a text, understanding explicit meaning
- Explore the use of articles *a* and *an*

Writing

- Use vocabulary relevant to a familiar topic
- Record answers to questions as a list
- Present text as a story map with captions and as a poster
- Write a simple sequence of actions
- Include relevant information when writing simple non-fiction texts
- Use basic language and features appropriate to a text type
- End sentences with a full stop
- Relate rhyme to shared spelling patterns
- Use articles *a* or *an* appropriately

Speaking and listening

- Talk in pairs, taking turns to speak and listen to others without interrupting
- Speak clearly, providing relevant information

Resources

- Student's Book pages 54–57
- Workbook pages 38–39
- Slideshows: *Fruit and vegetables; Dairy and eggs ; Chopping rhyme; Food rhyme*
- Audio files: *Fruit and vegetables; Dairy and eggs; Chopping rhyme; Food rhyme*
- PCM 29: *a* or *an*?

Student's Book page 54

Listening and speaking

Tell learners that they are going to read and find out about another food group – fruit and vegetables.

1 Ask learners to identify the heading on page 54 and invite a learner to read it. Invite learners to read the first two sentences and discuss. Then ask learners what else they might find out about fruit and vegetables. Give them time to look at the pictures and read the labels, the captions and the text. Learners work in pairs to read and find out as much information as they can. Monitor what strategies learners are using and how successfully they are using them.

Support: Work with a small group to help them with the text. Guide them by asking questions. For example:

- What do you think we are going to learn about on this page? (pointing to a picture of, for example, a banana)
- What is this a picture of?
- Is a banana a fruit or a vegetable?
- Can you show me the word that says 'banana'?

Bring the class together to read the text. Start by asking learners to read the labels for the fruit. Emphasise that the label matches the picture. Discuss the different vocabulary used: 'fruit', 'trees', 'vines', 'skins', 'peeled' and 'stones'. This will help learners to use the context when reading the text.

Invite learners to read the sentences about fruit, encouraging them to use strategies – phonics, picture and label clues, and context. Then use the same strategies to help learners to read about vegetables.

Follow up by asking learners what they have found out about fruit and vegetables from the pictures and the text. They should read the relevant part of the text again if they need to clarify anything.

Spend as much time as necessary on this activity, ensuring accurate decoding and understanding of the text.

2 Learners work in pairs and answer the questions. They have the opportunity to talk about fruit and vegetables, which ones they eat and like, and which ones they have tried and not liked.

Monitor learners' use of '*a*' and '*an*' when they are talking about fruit and vegetables.

Bring learners together to discuss the fruit and vegetables that they like with a focus on using *a* or *an* correctly, for example: a banana, an apple, an orange, a mango, an avocado, a peach. Write examples given and elicit from learners why 'a' is used sometimes and at other times 'an' is used.

Give learners PCM 29 and ask them to complete it to confirm their understanding.

Student's Book page 55

Reading and writing

1 Using the text on page 54 as a reference, learners complete the sentences. Remind them to use the text to find and check answers.

2 Before learners do the activity, recap which fruits have large stones and which fruits have skin that needs to be peeled before it is eaten.

3–4 These activities are similar to activities 1 and 2, but with the focus on vegetables.

Learners could learn the following rhyme about chopping vegetables at this point.

> Chop, chop, choppity, chop,
> Cut off the bottom and cut off the top.
> What we have left we will put in the pot.
> Chop, chop, choppity, chop.

5 In this activity, learners are asked to choose a fruit and write about it. Elicit from learners what things they might include in their writing. For example, where does it grow, has it a stone, is it juicy, has it skin, is the skin edible, is it eaten raw or cooked or both?

Give learners time to think about what they might write before asking some learners to say what they are going to write.

You should ask learners if there are any words that should be added to the word displays and add if appropriate. Remind learners to refer to word displays if needed, and to remember capital letters and full stops.

Extension: Make a simple pictograph or block graph to show learners' favourite fruit (or vegetable). Limit the number of fruits to six. Ask learners to choose which of the six fruits they like best and add a drawing of the fruit to the correct column of the graph. (The pieces of paper should be cut to suit the size of the graph.) Make sure they label the graph correctly and that they give it a heading to make its meaning clear. (See the Cambridge Primary

Mathematics curriculum framework for more information on this topic if necessary.)

Answers

1 healthy foods; trees, vines; peeled; stones

3 plants; parts

Workbook page 38

Writing

Before learners do the activity, give them the opportunity to make a fruit salad.

From a selection of fruit (real or pretend) ask what you need to do first, next and so on, eliciting the words 'peel', 'chop', 'mix' and 'eat'. Carry out each part of the task commenting on what you are doing. For example: 'First I peel the mango.' The activity has four parts to the instructions – first, next, then, last of all. Elicit from learners how these words help with the order.

Put learners in groups of four. Each person in the group is responsible for one part of the instructions. Give learners time to sequence the instructions before asking each group of four to report their instructions.

Learners should then complete the instruction framework. Again, some learners may benefit from you acting as scribe for this activity. This would allow you to assess if they can sequence events without getting caught up with handwriting and spelling. You could perhaps write the first two or three sentences in the sequence with them writing the rest.

Student's Book page 56

Reading

Tell learners that they are going to read and find out about another food group – dairy and eggs. Ask learners to point to the heading on page 56 and read it together. Then ask them to look at the pictures about milk. Give learners a little time to look at the pictures before asking them to describe each picture.

Discuss the pictures, highlighting words that appear in the text. Then give learners some time to read the text in pairs. Tell them that they will be reading about what happens to milk after it comes from a cow or another animal. Remind them about the strategies they have used previously when reading text.

Follow the same procedure for the part of the text that deals with dairy products and eggs. Then ask questions to check understanding. For example:

- What animals do we get milk from?
- What do we call the truck that takes the milk from the farm to the dairy?
- What foods are made from milk?

Spend as much time as necessary on this activity to ensure accurate decoding and understanding of the text.

Student's Book page 57

Reading and writing

1 This activity requires learners to use information from the text to complete and copy sentences about milk.

2 Before learners draw a story map, refer to the relevant pictures on page 56. Discuss what is happening in each picture and write some key words on the whiteboard.

Put learners in groups of three. Each learner in a group should take one part of the sequence that describes what happens from the time the cows are milked to the time the milk is bottled. The group then tell their story to their peers. After learners tell the story correctly, ask them to draw three pictures to show what happens to milk.

If further scaffolding for this task is necessary, provide learners with a story map template.

3 This activity asks learners to write captions under each picture.

Support: Some learners may need support to do this. The learner says what happens and the teacher scribes what happens.

4 Learners are asked to make a list of foods that are made from milk. Remind learners how a list is written.

5 Learners are asked to use information from the text to complete sentences about eggs.

6 Before learners complete the activity, discuss with them how ice cream is made and what makes one kind of ice cream different from another – flavour. Elicit different flavours of ice cream, for example chocolate, mint, strawberry and vanilla. (Learners may well come up with some very interesting flavours.) Learners may want to add toppings to their ice cream and they would have to include these in the ingredients.

7 Before learners make a poster, discuss with them what a poster is and what should be included on a poster about ice cream, for example size, prices and flavours. They should think of a good name for the ice cream shop where the ice cream will be sold.

Extension: 1 Learners could draw a picture of their new flavoured ice cream on paper. They could then cut out the picture and use it to make a display with labels and a heading.

2 Use this simple poem below as a model and ask learners to make up their own rhyming lines linking people's names with food. If they struggle, you could give them a list of foods as a starting point, for example egg, stew, peas, macaroni, cake, papaya and melon, and ask them to think of names that rhyme with each type.

For a project on food
I asked my friends "What is good?"
Betty said spaghetti,
Louise said cheese,
Murray said curry,
Anna said banana,
Ted said bread,
Sam said yam,
Trish said fish,
Sue said callaloo,
No, wait! Maybe stew.
What about you?

by Karen Morrison

Answers

1 milk; cows (goats and sheep)
5 chickens; boxes; sell

Workbook page 39

Sounds and spelling

Use the word 'egg' to highlight that some words in English end with a double consonant. Ask learners what they notice about the word 'egg' and highlight the double *gg*.

Highlight any other words with double consonants at the end that learners might know, for example 'add', 'bell' and 'class'. Tell learners that the two letters need to be written but only one sound is made. They should learn to read and spell words ending in *–ss*, *–ff* and *–ll*. Some learners will have investigated this in Unit 3.

Remind learners that consonant-vowel-consonant (CVC) words do not end in *–s*, *–f* or *–l*, with the exceptions of 'gas', 'bus', 'has' and 'his'.
(**Note:** The *s* in 'has' and 'his' sounds like *z*.) The mnemonic '**S**illy **f**oolish **l**etters, they don't stand on their own' might help learners to remember the rule.

The activity on Workbook page 39 asks learners to use the letters in the boxes to make new rhyming words ending in *–ff*, *–ss* and *–ll*. When they have finished the activity, invite learners to say what words they have made and highlight the double consonants.

Answers

cuff	less	pass
huff	mess	glass
puff	dress	brass
stuff	press	class

tell	hill	cross
bell	pill	toss
well	spill	moss
sell	frill	boss
smell	still	loss

Weekly review

Use this rubric to assess learners' progress as they work through the activities this week. You can use the activities suggested beneath the table to follow up on your on-going assessment.

Level	Reading	Writing
■	Can tell a sequence of sentences as instructions to make a fruit salad. After first instructions have been scribed, can write the rest.	Needs some support to work as a group of three or four to tell a sequence of events.
●	Can write a sequence of sentences as instructions to make a fruit salad, with minimal support.	Can work in threes or fours to tell a sequence of events. Needs some reminding about turn taking.
▲	Can write a sequence of sentences as instructions to make a fruit salad.	Can work in threes or fours to tell a sequence of events, taking turns to speak.

Support: Give support to learners to organise their thoughts, say aloud the sequence of instructions and support to write, scribing if appropriate.

Extension: Using the format 'First… Next… Then… Last of all', learners should write a sequence of instructions for another activity that they are familiar with, such as brushing their teeth or getting ready for school.

Week 3

Key strands and substrands: Lesson outcomes

Reading

- Read and understand an information text that includes pictures
- Answer questions about a text, understanding explicit meaning
- Use phonic knowledge to read decodable words and to sound out some elements of unfamiliar words
- Respond verbally to simple questions about texts read

Writing

- Record answers to questions as a list
- Present text as a labelled diagram
- Create a cover and contents page for a book, including relevant information
- Develop a simple sequence of actions

Speaking and listening

- Talk in pairs, taking turns to speak and listening to others without interrupting
- Speak clearly, providing relevant information
- Make simple personal statements

Resources

- Student's Book pages 58–60
- Workbook pages 40–41
- Slideshows: *Bread and cereals; Sugars and fats*
- Audio files: *Bread and cereals; Sugar and fats*
- PCM 30: End of unit task

Student's Book page 58

Reading

Tell learners that they are going to read and find out about another food group – bread and cereals.

Remind learners about the strategies they have used previously when reading text. Follow up by asking them about bread and cereals and encourage them to refer back to the pictures and text on page 58 to check the accuracy of answers.

Spend as much time as necessary on this activity to ensure accurate decoding and understanding of the text.

Student's Book page 59

Reading and writing

1 In this activity, learners use information from the text to complete sentences about bread.

2 In this activity, learners make a list of three different types of bread.

Answers

1. flour; wheat; fields
2. (possible answers) baguette, challah, croissant, naan, pitta

Listening and speaking

Elicit from learners the component parts of a sandwich, in other words, bread and a filling.

Before learners talk about making a sandwich, remind them to use words like 'first', 'next', 'then' and 'last of all'. They should then tell their peers how to make a sandwich. Learners should know that they will be asked to do this before working with their partner.

Working in pairs, learners tell each other what they like to put in a sandwich.

Support: Learners could report back in groups of four, with each learner having responsibility for one part of the instruction on how to make a sandwich.

Extension: Learners could report back on the discussion by writing 'How to make a sandwich' using a writing frame with the headings 'What I need' and 'What I do': First… Next… Then… Last of all…

Reading and writing

In this activity, learners use information from the text on page 58 to complete sentences about rice and then copy them.

Answers

shallow water; paddy fields

Listening and speaking

This activity gives learners the opportunity to talk in pairs about how rice is cooked and eaten in their home. This could be another opportunity for them to give a short presentation to their peers about how they eat rice at home. Remind learners to speak clearly and to show some awareness of the listener. Talk about things like looking at the audience, facial expression and body posture. Praise learners for good non-verbal communication.

Student's Book page 60

Reading and writing

This activity focuses on sugary and fatty foods. Discuss why it is important not to eat too many of them.

1 In this activity, learners draw and label some sugary and fatty foods.

2 In this activity, learners design a cover for a book about food. Remind them that a cover usually shows the reader what the content of the book will be about. Use non-fiction books from the class library to illustrate this and discuss what is on the cover – title, art work, author's name, illustrator's name.

3 In this activity, learners write a contents page for their food book. Again, use non-fiction books to illustrate how a contents page is laid out and show one on the whiteboard.

Discuss the sections in this unit and what each section is called. Ask questions like:

- How many sections are there?
- What is the first section about?
- What is the fourth section about?
- What page number will you write beside the section about fruit and vegetables?

Workbook page 40

Reading and writing

Read the instructions with learners and make sure that they understand what they have to do. Discuss with them what signs they might include, for example about prices, special offers and signs to encourage shoppers, such as 'Fresh Bread', 'BREAD BAKED TODAY'. Talk about what would be a good name for the stall.

Workbook page 41

Reading

In this section, learners decorate the border of a plate and draw a meal that they would like to eat. Remind them that the meal should be balanced and should include some of the foods they have learned about.

Thinking time

Invite learners to say what kinds of food they like and enjoy. Is what they eat always healthy? What makes some foods unhealthy? You need to be sensitive to what learners eat as they are not always in control of what type of food they eat!

Weekly review

Use this rubric to assess learners' progress as they work through the activities this week. You can use the activities suggested beneath the table to follow up on your on-going assessment.

Level	Reading	Writing
■	Knows the parts of a book and is aware that texts can look different. Can identify non-fiction texts.	Shows improvement when presenting to peers. Speaks more clearly and is better able to keep to the topic.
●	Knows the parts of a book and is aware that texts have different purposes and look different. Can identify non-fiction texts.	Speaks clearly and audibly when presenting to peers.
▲	Knows the parts of a book and is aware that texts have different purposes and look different. Can identify non-fiction texts.	Speaks clearly and audibly when presenting to peers. Chooses words carefully to express what they want to say.

Support: Give learners further opportunities to make short presentations to their peers. These could be to a wider audience, perhaps another class or at a school assembly. Learners could plan a presentation about what they have learned in this unit.

- Allow learners to choose what they would like to say.
- Allow learners to speak in pairs.
- Allow learners to say a few words perhaps holding a prop, for example a section title that reads 'Fruit and Vegetables'.
- Allow learners to have words written on cards as a prompt if necessary.

Extension: Learners could give the presentation as above. For extra challenge, remind them to look at the audience, to speak clearly and audibly, and about the difference in the way they need to speak at an assembly compared to speaking in their classroom, by projecting their voice.

End of unit task

Use PCM 30 to assess whether learners are able to find and record information about food groups. Hand out a copy of PCM 30 to each learner and ask learners to complete them. Tell them that they can use the information texts in the unit to find any answers that they do not know. Observe them as they work to make sure they know how to search efficiently for information using headings and the structure of the text.

Unit 7 Traditional stories

Unit overview

As learners work through this unit, they will read a story aloud and then retell and talk about the events in the story. *The Small Bun* is a story based on the traditional story, *The Gingerbread Man*.

The unit could follow on from listening to other traditional stories as part of learners' experience of listening to a range of books.

Learners will further develop their appreciation of direct speech in stories.

They will have the opportunity to make simple inferences about characters.

They will have the opportunity to read and write high-frequency words and other familiar words.

From Unit 7 onwards, learners are encouraged to record new, interesting or tricky words in a 'Word book'. Learners' Word books can take the form of a ruled notebook or the teacher can provide separate sheets of paper that can be kept in a folder.

Introducing the unit

Remind the class that you have read many stories to them and have a discussion about the different types of stories that you have read. Encourage learners to say which ones they liked and which they did not like. They should give reasons for their choices.

Bring the discussion round to traditional stories and invite learners to share the titles of any that they know, for example: *The Six Fools, How the Zebra Got its Stripes, The Lion and the Mouse, Jack and the Beanstalk* and the Anansi tales. Tell learners that they are going to read a story based on a traditional story called *The Gingerbread Man*. Explain that folk tales are popular stories that have been passed down from one generation to the next in the spoken form, before ever being written.

There are often many versions of the story and these versions differ from place to place, and the details change from culture to culture. Discuss why this might be. Ask learners if they know of any other folk tales, and talk about any they might have read or heard. Invite learners to say how many traditional stories begin, for example, 'Once upon a time…' or 'A long time ago…'. The stories often take place in a distant land and feature imaginary characters.

Week 1

Key strands and substrands: Lesson outcomes

Reading

- Identify parts of a book
- Read a traditional story and start to understand its characteristics
- Answer questions about a story and the characters and events in it
- Explore implicit meanings and make basic inferences about a text
- Identify the sound represented by the vowel digraph ‘ee’
- Begin to show understanding of sentences from a story and recognise a range of common words
- Explore and understand the use of articles *the* and *a* in sentences

Writing

- Record interesting words in a spelling log to extend vocabulary
- Practise joining letters, using a comfortable pencil grip
- Use articles *the* or *a* appropriately in sentence

Speaking and listening

- Listen to a story and think about questions
- Read aloud with expression, enacting the characters and pausing at full stops
- Suggest how someone's non-verbal communication reflects their feelings

Resources

- Student’s Book pages 61–66
- Workbook pages 42–43
- Slideshow: *The Small Bun*
- Audio files: *The Small Bun*
- PCM 31: Phonics *ee*

Student’s Book page 61

Reading and writing

Give learners time to look at the picture of the front cover of the book and ask them to read the instructions individually or in pairs. Then bring the class together and invite them to read aloud what they are being asked to do. Model correct reading and ensure that learners understand what is being asked of them before setting them to do the activity.

Bring learners together and talk about the discussion points as a class. Read the title of the book and ask if anyone knows what a ‘bun’ is. (A bun is a small bread or bread roll. Some buns are sweet. They come in different shapes and sizes but are most commonly hand-sized or even smaller, with a round top and a flat bottom.) Show learners some pictures of buns. Then invite them to say what they think the story is going to be about.

Answers

The Small Bun; Martin Waddell; fiction, because there is a cartoon image on the cover

Listening and reading

Play the audio file or read the story to learners.

Read the story again while learners follow in their books. This time, while they listen and follow the story, they need to think about the characters in the story.

- Who is the main character in the story?
- How many animal characters are in the story?
- What are their names?

Ensure that learners understand the questions before reading the story again by asking them what they need to think about while they listen to the story.

After you have read the story, invite learners to say what they have been listening for. They may give different answers, but encourage them to refer back to the story and find evidence for their answers if they disagree.

Answers

The small bun; three; sheep, goat, fox

Student’s Book pages 62–65

Reading and writing

1 Spend as much time as necessary on this section to ensure correct decoding of the text and to encourage reading with fluency. Monitor and assess the needs of different learners as they use strategies – phonic skills, context and grammatical clues, reading on and rereading – to work out any unknown words. Encourage them to read the story with expression. Remind them to pause when they see full stops in the story.

Support: Use records and ongoing assessment to determine the next steps for individual learners who are struggling.

2–4 Ask learners to read questions 2–4 in this section and check that they know what they have to do before they complete the activities. Ask them to explain their thinking in response to activity 4.

Answers

4 a hungry man; two; the small bun hopped off the dish and ran; possible answers include: cross, sad, worried

Workbook page 42

Reading and writing

Ask learners to read to page 62 in the Student's Book. Then ask: 'What did the sheep say?' Learners then work in pairs to find and read the words that the characters actually said. For example:

page 3

- Sheep: "Lunch! Yummy-yum!"
- Small bun: "I am too fast for the man and his wife, and I am too fast for you!"

page 11

- Small bun: "Why have you stopped?"

page 12

- Fox: "To eat you!"

Highlighter tape is useful here to highlight the words in the story that each character says.

Then invite pairs of learners to read aloud the words of a pair of characters. Encourage them to use different voices to suit the situation and the characters.

Now ask learners to do the activity, matching what the fox said with the picture of the fox, and what the small bun said with the picture of the small bun.

Answers

Small bun: I am too fast for the man and his wife; If I get on your back, you will eat me!; Why have you stopped?

Fox: You have beaten me; Trust me; To eat you!; Get on my back and I will carry you across the river.

Student's Book page 66

Sounds and spelling

This section focuses on two letters '*ee*' making one sound, as in 'feet', 'peel', 'sleep' and 'sheep'.

Tell learners that they need to listen for the sound in the middle of some words. Then say words like 'feet', 'keep', 'heel' and 'weed' and ask learners what sound they hear in the middle of each word. Confirm the long vowel sound *ee* and show how it is written, *ee*. Tell learners that there are other ways to write this sound and that they will learn about them soon.

Ask learners what kind of letter *e* is and confirm that they know it is a vowel. Explain that when two vowels come together, the first one usually sounds like its name and the other is silent. They should only say one *e* (name).

Here is a good rhyme to help learners to remember this rule:

When two vowels together play a game
Only the first one says its name.

Now say a word with *ee*, for example 'feel', and ask how many sounds learners can hear in 'feel'. Confirm that there are three sounds and invite learners to say what they are *(f-ee-l)*. Write the word 'feel' on the whiteboard.

Ask learners how to write 'peel', 'heel', 'reel', 'wheel' and 'steel' and write them in a list under 'feel'. Ask learners to read the list of words and ask what they notice about them. Confirm that they all have *ee* in the middle and they all end in *l* – they rhyme.

Repeat the above procedure for 'deep', 'keep', 'peep', 'weep', 'sheep', 'sleep', 'steep' and 'cheep'.

Here are some other words you could investigate, read and spell with the class:

'feet', 'need', 'leek'
'meet', 'seed', 'meek'
'sleet', 'weed', 'peek'
'sheet', 'greed', 'seek'
'sweet', 'tweed', 'week'
'feed', 'cheek'
'speed'.

Before learners do activities 1–3 in this section, check that they can identify the pictures and understand what they have to do. Ask learners to read aloud to check for accurate decoding and understanding of what is being asked.

PCM 31 gives further practice of writing words with *ee*. Check learners' pencil grip to ensure they can write efficiently and comfortably. Encourage them to try joining the letters *ee* when writing.

Dictation: Use these or similar sentences for dictation in this unit.

- We can feed the sheep.
- The bee is in the tree.
- I will go to the park next week.
- The wheel is in the shed.
- I need to meet my sister this week.
- She plants seeds and pulls out weeds.

Once learners have mastered the double *ee* sound, you could take the opportunity to ask them to identify if the vowel in the middle of words is a short *e* (sound) or a long *e* (name) in spoken words, for example: 'red', 'sleep', 'teeth', 'get', 'pet', 'sweet', 'bleed', 'pen', 'need', 'bed' and 'wheel'.

Answers

1 sheep; sweet; teeth

2 bee; tree; three

3 tree; bee; three

Workbook page 43

Reading and writing

1 Invite learners to read pages 3, 5 and 7 of the story. Focus on:

- 'a hungry sheep' / 'the sheep'
- 'a hungry goat' / 'the goat'
- 'a cunning fox' / 'the cunning fox'

Elicit the use of *a* and *the* with learners and discuss. Explain they should use *a* when referring to any member of a group, for example *a fox*. They should use *the* when referring to particular thing/person/animal, for example *the fox*.

The activity asks learners to complete sentences from *The Small Bun* using *a* or *the*.

2 This activity asks learners to complete a sentence from *The Small Bun*. The words given are all high-frequency words. Ongoing opportunities should be given to practise spelling high-frequency words.

Answers

1 The, the; A, the; The, the; The, a

2 for; his; the; you; said

Weekly review

Use this rubric to assess learners' progress as they work through the activities this week. You can use the activities suggested beneath the table to follow up on your on-going assessment.

Level	Reading	Writing
■	Can identify the words that characters speak in text with some support.	Can spell words with the long vowel phoneme *ee* in rhyming lists and in dictated sentences most of the time.
●	Can identify the words that characters speak in text.	Can spell words with the long vowel phoneme *ee* in dictated sentences and in own writing most of the time.
▲	Can identify the words that characters speak in text.	Can spell words with the long vowel phoneme *ee* in dictated sentences and in own writing.

Support: Work with a small group of learners to identify the words spoken by individual characters. Write on separate speech bubbles to assign the speech bubbles to the characters, fox, small bun, sheep or goat. Learners should then choose one speech bubble that has been assigned to the fox and one speech bubble assigned to another character, draw the characters, showing the scene that the dialogue comes from, and glue the speech bubbles to the correct character.

Extension: Learners should work in pairs, one being the fox and the other being either the small bun, the sheep or the goat. They should draw the two characters of their choice, write words that the characters said to each other in speech bubbles. Then cut the pictures and speech bubbles out and mount for display.

Week 2

Key strands and substrands: Lesson outcomes

Reading

- Identify the sounds represented by the vowel digraphs *ee* and *oa*
- Recognise a range of common words, including common exception words
- Understand sentences encountered in reading
- Identify the sequence of events in a story
- Explore the use of capital 'I' in a story
- Identify and record interesting and significant words

Writing

- Practise joining letters, using a comfortable pencil grip
- Relate rhyme to shared spelling patterns
- Read own writing aloud to check for sense and accuracy
- Begin to use some formulaic language
- In more extended writing, end some sentences with a full stop

Resources

- Student's Book pages 67–68
- Workbook pages 44–45
- PCM 32: Phonics *oa*
- PCM 33: Phonics *ai*
- PCM 34: Words with long vowels

Student's Book page 67

Sounds and spelling

This section focuses on two letters '*oa*' making one sound, as in 'goat'.

Tell learners that they need to listen for the sound in the middle of some words. Then say words like 'coat', 'boat', 'road' and 'soap' and ask learners what sound they hear in the middle of each word. Confirm the long vowel sound *o* and show how it is written, *oa*. Tell learners that there are other ways to write this sound and that they will learn about them soon.

Ask learners what kind of letter *o* is and confirm that they know it is a vowel. Remind them that when two vowels come together, the first one usually sounds like its name and the other is silent. Repeat the rhyme:

When two vowels together play a game
Only the first one says its name.

Now say the word 'goat' and ask how many sounds learners can hear in 'goat'. Confirm that there are three sounds and invite learners to say what they are *(g-oa-t)*. Write the word 'goat' on the whiteboard.

Ask learners how to write 'coat', 'moat', 'float', 'stoat' and 'throat', and write them in a list under 'goat'. Then ask them to read the list of words and ask what they notice about the words. Confirm that they all have *oa* in the middle and they all end in *t* – they rhyme.

Here are some other words you could investigate, read and spell with the class:

'coal', 'load', 'loan', 'toast'
'goal', 'road', 'moan', 'roast'
'foal', 'toad', 'boast'
'coast'.

Before learners do activities 1–3 in this section, check that they can identify the pictures and understand what they have to do.

Learners should have ongoing opportunities to practise joining the letters and writing words when you dictate them.

PCM 32 gives further practice writing words with *oa*.

Dictation: Use these or similar sentences for dictation in this unit.

- The soap is in the sink.
- We had toast and milk.
- We went on a coach to the zoo.
- The toad swam in the pond.
- The oak tree is big.

Tell learners that you are going to say some words, and ask them if the vowel in the middle of each word is a short *o* (sound) or a long *o* (name).

Suggested words: 'float', 'cot', 'stoat', 'coat', 'not', 'spot', 'cloak', 'soap', 'clot', 'toad'.

Once learners have done this, use the same procedure to teach two letters making one sound '*ai*' as in 'mail'.

Here are some other words you could investigate, read and spell with the class:

- 'fail', 'hail', 'nail', 'jail', 'mail', 'nail', 'pail', 'rail', 'sail', 'tail', 'snail', 'trail'
- 'laid', 'pain', 'raid'
- 'gain', 'rain', 'pain', 'stain', 'train', 'grain', 'brain', 'Spain', 'chain'
- 'wait', 'waist'
- 'paint', 'faint'.

PCM 33 gives practice writing words with 'ai'.

Dictation: These sentences are suitable for dictation as you work through this unit.

- We will wait for the train.
- Zack got wet feet in the rain.
- The snail is on the grass.
- The dog has a long tail.
- Mum will need red paint.

Answers

1 goat; boat; coat

2 road – toad; coast – toast; goal – foal; soak – cloak

3 coat, boat, moat; loan, moan, groan; coast, roast, boast

Workbook page 44

Sounds and spelling

Before learners do this activity, give them practice in identifying the sound that they hear in the middle of words. Say some words and ask learners if the sound in the middle is *ee* or *oa*. They could point to or hold up a card or piece of paper with the letters *ee* or *oa* written on them. Alternatively, they could write *ee* or *oa* when you say a word.

Suggested words: 'road', 'keep', 'boat', 'goal', 'peep', 'steep', 'float', 'fleet', 'feet', 'roast'.

In this section, learners choose *ee* or *oa* to complete words and then write the words. Again, check that learners can identify the pictures before they do the activity.

Answers

goal; feet; road; peel; heel; toad; tree; goat

Student's Book page 68

Reading and writing

1 Learners practise writing four high-frequency words that have appeared in the story. Learning to read and spell high-frequency words should be an ongoing activity.

2 Learners are asked to use the high-frequency words to complete and copy sentences from the story.

3 Learners start to investigate formulaic language in traditional stories, in the form of openings such as 'Once upon a time…'. Read the list of openers with them. Ask if they can think of any other ways that stories they have heard or read begin.

Learners then choose one of the openers and make up the first sentence of a story using it.

Extension: Ask learners how traditional stories end. What usually happens? What words and phrases can they think of that are often used in stories (for example, 'happily ever after').

Answers

2 have; me; my; you

Workbook page 45

Reading and writing

This activity involves learners imagining they are the small bun and telling its story.

1 Ask learners to work in pairs and tell the story from the point of view of the small bun. They need to tell the story with the events in the correct order. Encourage them to use the words 'first', 'next', 'then' and 'last of all'.

The learners then complete activity 1. It assesses if learners can retell the story and spell the words used. With the exception of 'table' and 'me' the words are consonant-vowel-consonant (CVC) words, or words with two letters representing one sound, as in 'dish', 'sheep', 'goat' and 'back'.

Draw learners' attention to the capital 'I'. Learners could highlight each capital 'I' on the page.

2 Learners read their story aloud and check that it makes sense.

Answers

man; dish; sheep; goat; fox; back; fox; me

Weekly review

Use this rubric to assess learners' progress as they work through the activities this week. You can use the activities suggested beneath the table to follow up on your on-going assessment.

Level	Reading
■	Can read words with the long vowel phonemes *ee, oa and ai* when the words are in a mixed order most of the time.
●	Can read words with the long vowel phonemes *ee*, *oa and ai* when the words are in a mixed order and in a reading context most of the time.
▲	Can read words with the long vowel phonemes *ee, oa and ai* when the words are in a mixed order and in a reading context.

Support: Create four 3 x 3 'bingo cards' with the following words on:
Bingo board 1: snail, float, roast, sleep, chain, week, steep, toad, rain
Bingo board 2: steep, road, chain, week, snail, roast, goat, speed, toad
Bingo board 3: steep, roast, chain, speed, drain, float, train, goat, soap
Bingo board 4: sleep, road, snail, train, speed, week, drain, rain, soap

Hand out the bingo cards and counters to 2–4 learners.
Call words from this list: snail, goat, float, roast, speed, sleep, chain, week, steep, toad, rain, road, drain, soap, train.
Learners should place a counter on the word called if it is on their board. The learner who covers all the called words correctly is the winner.

Extension: Give learners PCM 34. They are asked to read words with long vowels 'ee', 'oa', or 'ai' and match each word to its meaning. Encourage learners to read all words and all meanings before starting matching.

Week 3

Key strands and substrands: Lesson outcomes

Reading

- Read an instruction text (recipe)
- Identify the main characters in a story
- Make simple inferences based on a text
- Use phonic knowledge to read and sound out some elements of unfamiliar words
- Recognise a range of common words on sight, including common exception words
- Understand words and sentences encountered in reading

Writing

- Write a sequence of instructions
- Create a story map with captions
- Draw and write a new ending for a story
- Read own writing aloud and talk about it

Resources

- Student's Book pages 65, 69–70
- Workbook pages 46–47
- Slideshow: *Recipe for buns*
- Audio file: *Recipe for buns*
- PCM 35: End of unit task

Student's Book page 69

Reading and writing

Before learners do the activities in this section, remind them about the style of instruction texts using 'How to make a fruit salad' (see Unit 6) as an example. Discuss ingredients and instructions. Focus on the importance of the order of the instructions.

1 This activity focuses on a recipe for making buns: the ingredients needed and the method. Write the word 'ingredients' on the whiteboard and check that learners know what it means. Ask them what ingredients they might need to bake buns, for example flour, sugar, eggs and butter. Discuss what they would do with the ingredients to make the buns, focusing on the method in the activity. Use the recipe to discuss the ingredients and the equipment needed before learners read the recipe.

2 If possible, show learners recipe books and point out the layout of ingredients and method.

Learners then use the pictures as a guide to write the instructions (method) in the correct order. The recipe can be used as a visual aid.

Support: Ask learners to tell you the sequence of instructions as shown in the pictures. Then support them with writing.

Extension: Do a simple baking activity with learners.

Answers

Mix the ingredients well.
Put the mixture on to a baking tray.
Put the tray in the oven.
Take the tray out of the oven when the buns are ready.
Leave the buns to cool.

Workbook page 46

Reading

This section focuses on the feelings of the man and his wife when the bun ran away.

1 Ask learners to think about how the man and his wife might have felt when they sat down to eat the small bun, eliciting words like 'happy', 'hungry', and so on. Then ask how they might have felt when the bun ran away, eliciting words like 'cross', 'sad', 'worried', and so on. Write the words on the whiteboard.

Ask learners to do activity 1.

2 In this activity, learners draw a picture of the man and his wife as the bun hopped off the dish. Discuss what facial expressions the people might have, and encourage learners to try to draw the expressions.

Extension: Some learners could add speech bubbles to the characters and write what they might have said.

Answers

1 Learners' own answers

Student's Book page 70

Reading and writing

1 Learners are asked to write the names of the characters in the story.

2 Before learners do activity 2, ask them to think again about how the man and his wife felt when the small bun ran away and what they might have said. Then ask them to work in pairs, taking the roles of the man and his wife, and act out the scene. Learners then write what each character might have said.

3 Learners draw a story map of the small bun's meeting with the sheep, the goat and the fox. Discuss with learners what would be in each picture. For example, there might be a gate and grass in the picture with the sheep, a lane in the picture with the goat, and a river in the picture with the fox.

If further scaffolding for this task is necessary, provide learners with a story map template.

4 Learners write captions under each picture.

Support: Support learners by asking them to write one, two or three captions. Again, ask them to tell you what they are going to write first.

Extension: Put learners into groups. Each learner takes on the role of a character. The group then acts out the story. Remind learners of some of the things they have been learning about, for example using different voices, different facial expressions and speaking clearly.

Each group then gives a performance to the rest of their peers.

Answers

1 man, wife, small bun, sheep, goat, fox

Workbook page 47

Writing

Encourage learners to think of alternative endings to this story, for example the bun jumped into the river and found he could swim; someone came to help him; he persuaded the fox not to eat him.

Ask learners to share their alternative endings with a partner and then invite individuals to share them with the class. Praise learners' ideas and highlight good sentence structure and use of vocabulary. Say things like: 'I really like the way you started that sentence. That made me want to hear more of your new ending. Well done.'

Learners do the activity. They draw a picture to show their alternative ending and write a sequence of sentences telling the new ending. Remind learners to remember to use capital letters and full stops to start and end their sentences. Encourage learners to read their own writing before inviting some learners to read their writing to the class. Invite learners to say what they liked about the stories that have been read aloud.

Support: After individuals or small groups have drawn the new ending for their story, invite them to tell you the new ending before helping them to write it.

Thinking time

Invite learners to say how the hungry man and his wife could show how they felt without speaking when:

- he sat down with his wife to eat the small bun
- the small bun hopped of the dish and ran.

Discuss with learners how we don't have to say anything to let others know how we feel. What facial expressions and gestures tell others how we feel? What a difference a smile can make!

Weekly review

Use this rubric to assess learners' progress as they work through the activities this week. You can use the activities suggested beneath the table to follow up on your on-going assessment.

Level	Reading
■	Using the picture they have drawn, can tell a sequence of sentences to tell a new ending to a story. Then with support, write the new ending.
●	Can write a sequence of sentences to tell a new ending to a story. Uses some good vocabulary and spells most common words accurately.
▲	Can write a sequence of sentences to tell a new ending to a story. Uses relevant vocabulary and spells common words accurately.

Support: Reread a familiar story with learners and invite them to suggest how the ending could be changed. Discuss options and invite learners to say which one they would like to choose as the new ending for the story. Scribe the new ending on the whiteboard, modelling writing skills such as capital letters, spellings of high-frequency words and full stops.

Extension: Using a familiar story that you have read to learners, invite them to work in pairs to change the ending. Learners should then write the story ending.

End of unit task

Use PCM 35 to assess how well learners are able to form and write sentences. You may choose to observe learners as they work and to record your observations, or you could collect and mark their work, providing feedback and making notes about those who need further support in this area.

Unit 8 Feelings

Unit overview

As learners work through this unit they will read a story aloud, and then retell, talk about and sequence the events in the story. *The Lonely Penguin* is a story with a predictable structure and patterned language. Learners will also read facts from an information text (a fact file) about penguins.

They will have the opportunity to talk about both positive and negative feelings in a safe context and find ways of managing feelings.

The unit could be part of social and emotional development with a focus on what to do when you are feeling lonely or when you feel that you do not have friends.

Introducing the unit

The unit could be introduced by talking to learners about breaktimes at school. Ask questions to get the discussion started. For example: 'What do you play? Who do you sit/play with? How do you feel during breaktimes? Does anyone ever feel lonely?'

The Lonely Penguin fits well into a personal and social development programme, and all issues that arise from the discussion with learners must be addressed. It is very important to be sensitive to the feelings of those who do not seem to have any friends and to be aware of any teasing or unkindness that may arise during class discussions.

Week 1

Key strands and substrands: Lesson outcomes

Reading

- Recognise the parts of a book
- Read and find information in a simple story, including using visual elements
- Read verbs ending in *–ing*
- Explore examples of verbs in sentences
- Begin to show understanding of word and sentences encountered in reading
- Identify sentences in texts and understand grammar of statements, including the importance of verbs and word order
- Anticipate what happens next in a story

Writing

- Record answers to simple questions

Speaking and listening

- Speak clearly in pair discussions and show understanding of partner's opinion
- Use some relevant vocabulary to describe events and feelings
- Understand that non-verbal communication may reflect how someone feels

Resources

- Student's Book pages 71–76
- Workbook page 48
- Slideshow: *The Lonely Penguin*
- Audio files: *The Lonely Penguin*
- PCM 36: Words ending in *–ed* and *–ing*
- PCM 37: Words ending in *–ed* and *–ing*

Student's Book pages 71–74

Reading and writing

Ask learners to look at the picture of the front cover of the book and to read the questions. Take learners' suggestions as to what they think the book will be about. Ensure that learners know why this is likely to be a fiction book – the title and the artwork indicate this.

Ask learners what the cover might look like if it was a non-fiction book.

Extension: Petr Horáček is an award-winning author and illustrator. Learners may enjoy reading about him and his work and doing presentations on his books and his style. His own website contains links to his books as well as DVDs that learners can watch. There is also a list of his awards, a biography and a blog that he updates regularly.

Speaking and reading

1 Learners work in pairs to discuss why the penguin might be lonely. Then bring them together as a class so they can tell each other what they think the reason is.

Note: Encourage learners to speak clearly and audibly while being sensitive to the fact that answers, and the way a learner speaks, could reflect how a learner may be feeling.

2 Before asking learners to read the story, go through it with them, asking them to describe what is happening in each picture. Are learners able to predict the text and what the story will be about from the pictures? Are the pictures a good match for the text? Highlight any vocabulary that comes from looking at the pictures and that appears in the text and write it on the whiteboard, for example: 'lonely', 'penguin', 'friends', 'snow', 'frost', 'ice', 'running', 'sliding', 'climbs', 'cold water' and 'swimming'. This will familiarise learners with the vocabulary and what happens in the story before they read.

Give learners time to read the story. Monitor how they are using phonics, and picture and context clues to work out any unknown words.

Support: It may be necessary to work with individuals to help them use strategies to read the text. Alternatively, put learners in groups and have them listen to the audio file as they follow the story.

Bring learners together and invite individuals to read aloud while the others follow.

Spend as much time as necessary on this activity to ensure correct decoding of the text and to encourage reading with fluency. Encourage learners to use a variety of strategies – phonic skills, picture, context and grammatical clues, reading on and rereading – to work out any unknown words.

3 After reading the story, learners are asked to talk about why the penguin was lonely. Was it what they thought before they read the story? Encourage them to articulate their reasons.

Student's Book page 75

Reading and writing

1 Learners look at the pictures and say what the penguin *is doing*. For example: 'Penguin *is looking* for his friends.'

Explore the text with learners to identify nouns and verbs. Highlighter tape is good for this activity. Elicit from learners that some of the verbs end in *–ing* and others in *–s*. Then invite learners to reread the text aloud, showing understanding of capital letters and full stops to indicate sentences and simple grammatical links between words, For example: [Penguin] [is looking] [for his friends]. Discuss with learners the importance of word order in sentences. Would the sentence make sense if written in a different order? Word order determines the sense of the sentence.

Learners then read all the sentences and write the one that matches each picture.

2 Remind learners that all the statements in the previous activity were sentences. They began with a capital letter and ended with a full stop. Learners then answer the question to practise identifying sentences in texts.

Extension: You could refer back to the story in this unit and identify sentences that end with punctuation other than a full stop. Can learners identify a question mark and an exclamation mark?

Answers

1 Penguin is looking for his friends.
Penguin is running through the snow.
Penguin is sliding on the frosty ice.
Penguin climbs up the hill.

2 six words; eight sentences

Student's Book page 76

Reading and writing

This section focuses on the suffix *–ing*.

1 This activity asks learners to find words ending in *–ing* in the story, *The Lonely Penguin*. Model how to do this in a systematic way. Ask learners to turn to page 1 of the text and point to any word ending in *–ing*. Show on the whiteboard how learners should write the page number and the word they find: 'Page 1 coming'. Ask learners to check if there are any words ending in *–ing* on page 2. Turn to page 3 and repeat the procedure. Then show learners how to write 'Page 3' under 'Page 1' and write the word 'looking' alongside, forming a list.

Learners do the activity. Monitor how they tackle it and assist any learners who seem to be struggling or disorganised. Observe whether:

- confident readers can scan the text to find the words
- some readers need to read every word on the page before identifying the *–ing* word
- some learners do a bit of both.

2 Before learners do the activity, give them an opportunity to add *–ing* to words. At this stage, use only words whose root does not change when *–ing* is added. Write the root word and then add *–ing* to make the new word on the whiteboard. For example:

'lift' + *–ing* = 'lifting'
'send' + *–ing* = 'sending'
'crush' + *–ing* = 'crushing'

3 Ask learners to use the *–ing* words in the box to complete sentences from the text.

Answers

1 Page 1 coming; Page 3 looking; Page 5 running; Page 6 sliding; Page 7 looking; Page 11 swimming
2 looking; fishing; keeping; cooking; crashing; peeping; hooking; brushing; sleeping
3 sliding; swimming; running

Workbook page 48

Reading

This activity assesses learners' reading of familiar text in a different tense from the story in the Student's Book.

Before learners start the activity, investigate the word ending *–ed*. Do this orally and ask learners to change from the present tense verbs to the past tense. For example:

Penguin is climbing up the hill. Yesterday penguin _______up the hill.

Penguin is looking for his friends. Yesterday penguin __________ for his friends.

Today I am painting. Yesterday I ____________.

Today I am walking. Yesterday I ____________.

Learners are asked to circle the verbs ending in *–ed* and then to draw lines to match the beginning of each sentence with its ending. Read the instructions with learners to check that they know what they have to do and that they realise there are two parts to the activity.

Answers

Penguin climbed up the hill.
Penguin looked for his friends.
Penguin laughed with his friends.
Penguin splashed in the cold water.
Penguin jumped into the air.

Weekly review

Use this rubric to assess learners' progress as they work through the activities this week. You can use the activities suggested beneath the table to follow up on your on-going assessment.

Level	Reading
■	Recognises the common word endings *–ed* and *–ing*.
●	Recognises the common word endings *–ed* and *–ing*. Can spell some words ending in *–ing* where *–ing* is added to the root word.
▲	Recognises the common word endings *–ed* and *–ing*. Can spell many words ending in *–ing* where *–ing* is added to the root word.

Support: Use PCM 36 to reinforce and assess work on different word endings.

Extension: Use PCM 37 to challenge learners in practising these endings, including creating their own sentences.

Week 2

Key strands and substrands: Lesson outcomes

Reading

- Identify the sounds represented by the digraphs *oo, ee* and *ow*
- Retell a story verbally, identifying the sequence of events
- Record interesting words to inform own writing
- Identify the characteristics of simple stories

Writing

- Practise joining letters, using a comfortable pencil grip
- Record interesting words in a spelling log to extend vocabulary
- Relate rhyme to shared spelling patterns
- Create a story map with captions
- Write a simple retelling of a story in a logical order, then read it aloud to check for sense

Speaking and listening

- Work well in pairs, listening without interrupting

Resources

- Student's Book pages 77–78
- Workbook pages 49–51
- PCM 38: Phonics *oo*

Student's Book page 77

Sounds and spelling

This section focuses on two letters making one sound '*oo*', as in 'moon'.

Tell learners that they need to listen for the sound in the middle of some words. Then say words like 'room', 'cool', 'spoon' and 'broom' and ask learners what sound they hear in the middle of each word. Confirm the long vowel sound *oo* and show how it is written, *oo*. Tell learners that there are other ways to write this sound and that they will learn about them soon.

Now say the word 'cool' and ask how many sounds learners can hear in 'cool'. Confirm that there are three sounds and invite learners to say what they are (*c-oo-l*). Write the word 'cool' on the whiteboard.

Ask learners how to write 'pool', 'fool' and 'stool' and write them in a list under 'cool'. Ask learners to read the list of words and ask what they notice about them. Confirm that they all have *oo* in the middle and they all end in *l* – they rhyme.

Here are some other words you could investigate, read and spell with the class:

- 'moon', 'soon', 'noon', 'spoon'
- 'toot', 'hoot', 'root', 'shoot'
- 'room', 'zoom', 'broom', 'bloom', 'groom', 'gloom'

Before learners do the activities, ensure that they can read the instructions and that they know what they have to do.

PCM 38 gives further practice in writing words with *oo*.

Dictation: Use these or similar sentences for dictation to reinforce the spellings taught in this and previous units. The sentences include words with *ee* in the middle.

- Mum has a big spoon.
- Nick is on the stool.
- I will go to the zoo next week.
- Lee took the wheel to the shed.
- We get wool from sheep.
- Adeel will meet us soon.
- The crab is in the deep pool.

Answers

2 moon; spoon; stool

3 hoop, loop, stoop; cool, tool, stool, pool; room, zoom, broom

Workbook page 49

Sounds and spelling

Before learners do this activity, give them practice in identifying the sound that they hear in the middle of words. Say some words and ask learners if the sound in the middle is *ee* or *oo*. They could point to or hold up a card or piece of paper with the letters *ee* or *oo* written on them. Alternatively, they could write *ee* or *oo* when you say a word.

Suggested words: 'cool', 'keep', 'room', 'moon', 'sheep', 'sleep', 'broom', 'sheet', 'week', 'spoon'.

In this section, learners write words with *oo* or *ee* in the middle. Check that learners can identify the pictures before they do the activity.

Answers

boot; feet; week; hoop; wheel; spoon; stool; sleep

Workbook page 50

Sounds and spelling

In Unit 7, learners learned about *oa* representing the long vowel sound *o* in the middle of words. This section focuses on the vowel sound represented by *ow* at the end of words.

Tell learners that they need to listen for the sound at the end of some words. Say words like 'snow', 'blow', 'show' and 'grow' and ask learners what sound they hear at the end of each word. Confirm the long vowel sound *o* and show how it is written, –*ow*, when it is at the end of a word.

Note: *ow* is the usual representation of the long vowel sound *o* when it is at the end of a single-syllable word. The exception is *oe,* as in 'toe', 'foe', 'doe', 'hoe', 'woe' and 'roe'.

Now say the word 'bow' and ask how many sounds learners can hear. Confirm that there are two sounds and invite learners to say what they are (*b-ow*). Write the word 'bow' on the whiteboard.

Ask learners how to write 'mow', 'row', 'sow' and 'tow' and write them in a list under 'bow'. Ask learners to read the list of words and say what they notice about them. Confirm that they all have –*ow* at the end – they rhyme.

Repeat the procedure for 'snow', 'blow', 'crow', 'flow', 'grow' and 'show'. Draw learners' attention to the consonant clusters at the beginning of 'blow', 'crow', 'flow' and 'grow' and the two letters making one sound at the beginning of 'show'.

Learners now do the activity on Workbook page 50. Check that they can read the instructions and understand what is being asked of them.

Dictation: Use these or similar sentences for dictation to reinforce the spelling taught in this and previous units.

- The snow is deep.
- A crow is black.
- The seeds will grow in pots.
- The stool is low.
- The wind will blow the flag.
- The clock is slow.

To build on this work, ask learners if they know what are the two different ways of making the long vowel sound *o*, and confirm *oa* and *ow*. If the long vowel sound *o* is in the middle of words, how is it usually written? Confirm *oa*. This applies to single-syllable words. (Exceptions are 'own', 'bowl' and 'grown'.) If the long vowel sound *o* is at the end of words, it is usually written *ow*. (Exceptions are 'toe', 'foe', 'hoe' and 'Joe'.)

Give learners the opportunity to identify the correct representation of the long vowel sound *o* in words. They could point to or hold up a card or piece of paper with letters *ow* or *oa* written on them. Alternatively, they could write *ow* or *oa* when you say a word.

Suggested words: 'coat', 'low', 'goal', 'loaf', 'blow', 'snow', 'boast', 'grow', 'moat', 'crow', 'toast', 'cloak', 'goal', 'float', 'show', 'flow', 'boat', 'row', 'coal', 'bow', 'goat', 'road', 'moan', 'tow', 'cloak', 'soap'.

Answers

2 grow; slow; blow; glow; flow; throw

3 window; rainbow; pillow

Student's Book page 78

Speaking

Before learners do the activity, give them the opportunity to work in pairs and retell the story. Then bring the class together to recap the sequence of events in the story:

- Penguin looking for his friends
- Penguin running through the snow
- Penguin sliding on the frosty ice
- Penguin climbing up the hill
- Penguin jumping into the air
- Penguin finding his friends.

Reading and writing

In this section, learners are asked to draw a story map to show the sequence of events of the penguin looking for and finding his friends. They are then asked to write captions for the pictures.

You could organise learners into groups of three for this activity, with each learner in a group taking responsibility for one picture. The pictures could be mounted in sequence for display. Learners could then discuss the captions before writing them.

If further scaffolding for this task is necessary, provide learners with a story map template.

Workbook page 51

Reading and writing

This section involves learners imagining that they are the penguin telling his story by completing sentences that are in sequence.

Remind learners to read what they have written and check that it makes sense. Alternatively, they can read and check a partner's work.

Support: You may need to provide the words for some learners to use.

Answers

(possible answers) my friends; snow; frosty ice; everywhere; hill; the air; my friends

Extension: Learners could write a 'Once upon a time…' story about a toy penguin. Discuss and elicit ideas about an adventure that the toy penguin might have. Talk about what the story should include: a character (a toy penguin), a setting (where is the action going to take place) and action (what happens to the penguin). Write some suggested vocabulary on the whiteboard. Learners could add some of these words to their Word books that might be useful for learners' writing.

Support: Some learners may need you to scribe their story.

Weekly review

Use this rubric to assess learners' progress as they work through the activities this week. You can use the activities suggested beneath the table to follow up on your on-going assessment.

Level	Reading	Writing
■	Uses phonics knowledge to read decodable words, including sounds represented by more than one letter.	Can retell a familiar story and, with support, write sentences to caption pictures.
●	Uses phonics knowledge, including long vowel phonemes to read decodable words.	Can retell a familiar story and write sentences to caption pictures.
▲	Uses phonics knowledge, including long vowel phonemes, to read decodable words and to attempt to sound out elements of unfamiliar words.	Can retell a familiar story and can confidently write sentences to caption pictures.

Support: After discussion about two or three previously unfamiliar pictures, invite learners to choose one picture and write a sentence about it.

Extension: Using a series of three pictures as prompts, learners should write a short story showing a beginning, middle and ending.

Week 3

Key strands and substrands: Lesson outcomes

Reading

- Read a fact file
- Answer questions with reference to a text
- Explore implicit meanings and make inferences
- Begin to link contexts and events in stories to real life
- Recognise the different features of fiction and non-fiction texts
- Make choices about what to read

Writing

- Present texts in different ways
- Record answers to simple questions about texts
- Use appropriate language, features and relevant information when creating a poster

Speaking and listening

- Use some relevant information to describe feelings
- Listen to a partner without interrupting, showing understanding of opinions
- Make simple personal statements
- Talk about own activities, expressing preferences

Resources

- Student's Book pages 79–80
- Workbook pages 52–53
- Slideshow: *Fact file: Penguins*
- Audio file: *Fact file: Penguins*
- Short film about penguins (teacher to source)
- PCM 39: End of unit task

Workbook page 52

Listening and speaking

1–2 Give learners time to talk before bringing them together for a class discussion about how the penguin might have felt when he found his friends. Then discuss what makes learners happy. Elicit from learners how their facial expression and body language can indicate how they are feeling. Highlight some vocabulary that could be used in the next section and write it on the whiteboard. Learners might want to add some words to their Word book.

Writing

Learners write six things around the happy face that make them feel happy.

Workbook page 53

Writing

Take the opportunity to highlight how the context of the story could be very similar to what might happen in real life. Ask learners to discuss how they could help anyone in school who might be feeling lonely. One suggestion could be to make a poster. Discuss what would be on the poster and how it would need to look to attract attention. It would be helpful to show a selection of posters to learners to illustrate features such as clear presentation, bold uncluttered pictures, style, colour and size of print.

Student's Book page 79

Reading

Discuss with learners how the penguin in the story *The Lonely Penguin* is a character in a story. Then tell them that they are going to watch a short film and read about real penguins. There are a number of documentary films about penguins on the internet. National Geographic has some good suitable videos, as do the BBC and other broadcasters. Choose one that is suitable for your class and watch it before you show the class to make sure nothing inappropriate is included.

Encourage learners to jot down notes as they watch to remind them of any interesting or surprising facts. After watching the film, discuss the key points and ask questions to check what information learners have found out from watching it.

Tell learners that they are going to work in pairs and read a fact file about penguins. Tell them that after they have read the fact file, they should be able to tell the class two facts (one fact each) about penguins. Encourage learners to look at the photographs to get as much information from them before they read the text. Remind learners to look back at the photographs if they are having difficulty with a word. This, along with other strategies, can help them.

Support: Peer support, where a confident reader works with a less confident reader, would be a good strategy to use here. Make sure that both readers become involved in the reading.

Student's Book page 80

Reading and writing

1 Learners work individually or in pairs. Ask them to read the fact file on page 79 again.

2–3 Ask learners to read the questions and make sure they understand what is being asked of them. Remind them to check their answers in the text. In activity 2, if a sentence is true, they should be able to show the evidence for their answer in the fact file.

Say two statements about penguins or write the statements on the board. (There must be evidence for the statements in the fact file.) For example:

- Penguins eat fish. (true – fourth sentence in the fact file on page 79)
- Small penguins live in colder climates. (false – seventh sentence in the fact file on page 79)

Ask learners if the first statement is true. Then ask learners to find evidence for their answer in the text. Do the same for the second statement.

Ask learners to do activities 2 and 3. Monitor how well learners do them. Do they refer back to the fact file to check answers and spelling?

Support: Support individuals as necessary with this activity. Peer support may be a good strategy for some learners.

Answers

2 Penguins are birds.
Penguins can swim.
The smallest penguin is the little blue.

3 fish and other small sea creatures; wings; seawater; emperor penguin; chick

Extension: Explore with learners how the features of *The Lonely Penguin* and the fact file are different.

Thinking time

Discuss with learners which text they preferred – the story about a penguin or the fact file on penguins. Encourage them to give reasons for their preferences. Talk about the pictures in each text type and whether they affected the learners' preferences.

Weekly review

Use this rubric to assess learners' progress as they work through the activities this week. You can use the activities suggested beneath the table to follow up on your on-going assessment.

Level	Reading
■	Speaks well, taking turns to speak in pairs or in a small group situation.
●	Speaks clearly, taking turns to speak, in pairs or in a larger group, or in a class situation. Shows some awareness of the listener.
▲	Speaks clearly, taking turns to speak, in pairs or in a larger group, or in a class situation. Shows awareness of the listener.

Extension/support: In groups of three or four, ask learners to think about what they have learned in Unit 8. Monitor the groups and support learners where appropriate, helping them to talk about the different types of activities, for example reading, writing, watching, listening and talking. Encourage them to talk about what they enjoyed. For example:

- I liked reading *The Lonely Penguin*.
- I liked working in a group and talking.
- I liked making the poster.
- I liked answering questions.

Learners should work in mixed groups with support as appropriate.

End of unit task

Use PCM 39 to assess phonic awareness and spelling skills. Hand out copies of the sheet for learners to complete. Display the answers and have learners check and correct each other's work.

Unit 9 Life lessons

Unit overview

As learners work through this unit, they will read a story aloud and then retell and talk about the events in the story. *Anansi and Turtle* is a traditional African folktale about the trickster spider, Anansi. The story is set in a familiar context. It deals with valuable life lessons about being fair and sharing with others, and showing respect for guests. Learners will have the opportunity to make simple inferences about characters and their behaviour.

Introducing the unit

The unit could be introduced by talking to the learners about when they might invite guests to their house and how the family would greet them. This could be an opportunity to look more closely at the different country's traditional greetings.

Week 1

Key strands and substrands: Lesson outcomes

Reading

- Listen to and read a traditional tale
- Answer questions to identify characters and events in a story
- Explore implicit meanings and make inferences, drawing on the text to explain thinking
- Explore word order in sentences
- Identify the sounds represented by more than one letter
- Use phonic knowledge to read and sound out words
- Anticipate what a story will be about
- Record interesting words from texts
- Explore sounds and words, and understand rhyme in a text
- Read verbs ending in *–s*

Writing

- Record answers to simple questions about texts
- Describe a character in a story
- Use organisational features appropriate for a piece of writing
- Relate rhyme to shared spelling patterns
- Write simple sentences
- Use a capital letter for proper nouns

Speaking and listening

- Work in pairs, expressing and listening to opinions

Resources

- Student's Book pages 81–86, 88
- Workbook pages 54–55
- Slideshow: *Anansi and Turtle*
- Audio file: *Anansi and Turtle*

Workbook page 54

Reading and writing

1 Before learners read the book, ask them to look at the cover and think about what the book is going to be about. Ask them to read the instructions of activity 1 before they circle the words that they think might describe what the book will be about. Remind learners that it is important to read all the words first and that they need to circle more than one word.

Bring the class together and invite them to say which words they circled. Follow up by asking questions, for example: 'What makes you think that word tells you what the book might be about?' Such questions encourage learners to use the picture to make sensible suggestions and not just choose words randomly. Discuss singular and plurals, for example a spider /spiders and why in this case, 'a spider' would be the better option to circle.

2 Learners write the plural forms of words from the story.

3 This activity asks learners to find words ending in *–s* and *–ed* in the story *Anansi and Turtle*. Model how to do this in a systematic way. Ask learners to turn to picture 1 of the text and point to any word ending in *–s*. Show on the board how learners should write the picture number and the word they find. You could also copy the text and let learners use markers or highlighter tape if this is available. Let learners read the sentence in which the word occurs aloud. (Omit the word 'potatoes' as this ends in *–es*.)

Then do the same with words that end in *–ed*. Learners can work alone or in pairs to do this. (Omit the words 'replied', 'lived' and 'piled'.)

When learners have completed the activity, bring the class together to discuss and clarify answers.

Answers

2 spiders, turtles, hands, coats, hats, visitors

3 *–s*: picture 1 visitors, guests; picture 3 hands; picture 4 beans, dumplings; picture 5 plates; picture 9 foods, peas, drops; picture 10 pockets, stones; picture 11 manners
–ed: picture 2 opened, asked; picture 5 returned, asked, answered; picture 6 tricked; picture 9 shouted; picture 10 jumped; picture 11 floated; picture 12 climbed, watched, tricked, sighed

Student's Book pages 81–83

Reading and listening

Play the audio file or read the story to learners. Then tell learners that you are going to read it again. This time they need to listen for the answers to the following questions:

- How many characters are in the story?
- What are the names of the characters?

Check that learners found the answers to the questions through listening.

Ask learners to read the story in pairs or individually. They then read it aloud to you. You can ask different learners to read parts of the story whilst the others follow.

Spend as much time as necessary on this section to ensure correct decoding of the text and to encourage reading with fluency. Encourage learners to use a variety of strategies, for example phonic skills, picture and context clues, reading on and rereading, to work out any unknown words.

Ask questions to check understanding. For example:

- What was Anansi doing when he heard a loud knock at the door?
- Why did Turtle have to wash his hands?
- Why did Turtle go home?
- Who sent the invitation to Anansi?
- Why did Anansi not sink when he first jumped into the water?
- What did Anansi do to help him get to the bottom of the pond?

Student's Book page 84

Reading and writing

1 Before learners read pages 1–4 of *Anansi and Turtle*, talk about the characters and their relationship to each other – they are likely to be friends. Elicit from learners who else would visit them, for example uncle, aunt, cousin, grandmother.

2–5 Invite learners to read the instructions for activities 2, 3 and 4 aloud and check that they all understand what is being asked.

Before they work on the activities, explain to learners that we cannot write words in any order. To make sense, the words in a sentence must come in a particular order. The *subject* (noun) will be *doing* something (verb). Remind the learners that sentences start with a capital letter and end with a full stop.

Ensure that for activity **5**, learners understand that not all of the words in the box are suitable to write in the list, and that they can also add some words of their own.

Extension: Learners could write the names of the people they live with and what their relationship is to them, for example mother, father, brother, sister, aunt, uncle, cousin, grandmother and grandfather. Remind learners to use a capital letter at the beginning of each name.

Answers

1 Anansi; Turtle

2 Anansi stuffed food into his mouth.
There was plenty of food on Anansi's table to share.
Turtle walked to Anansi's house.

3–4 There was a loud knock on the door; He floated to the top of the water; He climbed out of the pond.

5 For example: greedy, mean, hungry, unkind

Workbook page 55

Reading and writing

1 Learners can work in pairs and read the words, which are from the poem about mice in the Student's Book on page 88.

2 Learners select the words that rhyme and write them in the columns, as shown in the example.

3 Learners use words from the poem and add their own words that rhyme.

4 Learners read their lists out loud in their pairs.

Answers

2 mouse/house, stew/too, mice/nice

3 (suggestions) meal: feel, seal; make: bake, take, rake; light: fight, might, night, bite

Student's Book page 85

Reading, speaking and writing

1 Give learners time to read the whole story and then to talk about how they think Turtle felt when he arrived at Anansi's house and then after he left Anansi's house.

Bring the class together to discuss their answers and ask them to read the sentence(s) that made them think the way they do.

2 In this activity, learners are asked to write two lists of food. One list of food that Anansi ate and the other a list of food that they might give a friend who was coming to dinner. Invite learners to give suggestions for this list. Write some suggestions on the whiteboard. Learners may want to add some of the words to their Word book.

Learners are then asked to find and write the sentence that tells them that Turtle was hungry when he left Anansi's house.

3 Learners are asked to read the words in the box. Some of the words might describe how Turtle felt when he left Anansi's house. They are asked to draw a picture of Turtle, write his name and write a list of words to describe how Turtle felt when he left Anansi's house.

Answers

1 possible answers: happy, hungry; "Mmm! What a lovely smell. Can I join you for dinner?"; possible answers: Anansi tricked Turtle to go and wash his hands; Anansi ate all of the food because he did not want to share; "Oh Turtle, your hands are dirty. You cannot eat food with dirty hands"; "Turtle walks slowly," thought Anansi. "I have time to eat."

2 rice, beans, sweet potatoes, beef, dumplings; 'Turtle left with an empty tummy.'

3 For example: sad, upset, tearful, angry, hungry

Student's Book page 86

Sounds and spelling

This section focuses on the long vowel *i* represented by *y*.

Tell learners that they need to listen for the sound at the end of some words. Then say words like 'my', 'by', 'shy' and 'cry' and ask learners what sound they hear at the end of each word. Confirm the long vowel sound *i*.

Ask learners which letters they have already learned about make the long vowel sound *i* and confirm *igh*. Explain that there is another way to write this sound: *y*. Tell learners that if the long vowel sound *i* is in the middle of a word, it is usually represented by *igh*, but if it is at the end of the word, it is represented by *y*. Exceptions are 'die', 'lie', 'pie', 'tie' and 'vie'.

Tell learners you want to write the word 'my' and ask how many sounds they can hear in the word. Confirm that there are two sounds and invite learners to say what they are (*m-y*). Write the word 'my' on the whiteboard, saying: 'The first sound is *m* and this is how we write it. The second sound is *i* and this is how we write it when it is at the end of a word: *y*. The word is "my".'

Ask learners how to write 'by', 'cry', 'dry', 'fry' and 'try'. Remember to draw their attention to the consonant clusters in 'cry', 'dry', 'fry' and 'try'.

Repeat the above procedure for 'fly', 'sly', 'sky', 'sty', 'spy', 'shy' and 'why'.

Give learners practice in identifying the correct representation of the long vowel sound *i*. Say some words and ask learners if the *i* sound is represented by *igh* or *y*. They should point to/hold up a card or piece of paper with the letters representing the sounds *igh* and *y* written on them. Alternatively, they could write *igh* or *y* when you say a word.

Suggested words: 'night', 'shy', 'cry', 'tight', 'bright', 'light', 'why', 'by', 'flight', 'fly', 'fright', 'my', 'try', 'might', 'right', 'sky'.

Ask learners to read the instructions for activities 1–4. Check that learners can read and understand what is being asked of them before they do the activities.

Dictation: Use these or similar sentences as dictation to reinforce and assess the spelling rules taught in this unit.

- There is a fly on the cake.
- My mum went to see my gran.
- We will fry the fish for tea.
- Why did you cry?
- The class will try to sing the song.

Answers

2 my; cry; by; dry; try; fly; spy; sky; shy

Weekly review

Use this rubric to assess learners' progress as they work through the activities this week. You can use the activities suggested beneath the table to follow up on your on-going assessment.

Level	Reading	Writing
■	Can read familiar text aloud and takes some notice of full stops when reading.	Can write words in a list and, with support, can choose an appropriate heading to write.
●	Can read aloud, pausing at full stops when reading.	Can independently write words in a list and, with minimal support, choose and write an appropriate heading.
▲	Can read aloud independently, pausing at full stops when reading.	Can independently write words in a list and write an appropriate heading.

Support: Give learners the opportunity to suggest headings for lists of words, for example lists of current television programmes, lists of current films, lists of vegetables, shopping lists, types of cars, songs.

Extension: Give learners opportunities to choose a book and read a page silently, focusing on pausing at full stops, then to read it aloud before reading it to an audience. Remind learners about speaking clearly and audibly and with expression.

Week 2

Key strands and substrands: Lesson outcomes

Reading

- Find nouns in sentences
- Explore the use of *and* in sentences
- Read a poem and answer questions about it
- Find nouns, verbs and rhyming words in a poem
- Show understanding of sentences encountered in reading
- Join in with some words and phrases when reading poems

Writing

- Record answers in lists
- Use *and* to join clauses in sentences
- Include relevant information when writing a non-fiction text

Speaking and listening

- Read a poem aloud, showing awareness of rhythm

Resources

- Student's Book pages 82, 87–88
- Slideshow: *Mouse poem*
- Audio: *Mouse poem*
- Workbook pages 56–57

Student's Book page 87

Reading and writing

Take this opportunity to revise nouns (see Unit 5).

1 Learners are asked to find nouns in sentences and write them in a list.

2 Before learners do activity 2, invite them to say sentences about food that they like to eat. The sentences must contain the word *and*. You should write a few of the learners' sentences on the whiteboard. As you write, ask: 'What do I need to start the sentence with and what do I put at the end of the sentence?' Check whether the sentences have the word *and* in them.

Learners should read aloud one of their sentences for peer assessment.

Answers

1 Anansi, door, friend, Turtle; rice, beans, sweet potatoes, beef, dumplings

Workbook page 56

Reading

This activity assesses learners' reading of familiar text in a different setting from the story in the Student's Book.

Learners are asked to draw lines to match the beginning of each sentence with its ending. Read the instructions with learners to check that they know what they have to do.

Answers

"You were too slow and I was hungry."
Anansi did not like visitors at dinner time.
Anansi opened the door.
Turtle went to wash his hands.
Anansi began to eat the food.
"Why did you not wait for me?"
Anansi the spider sat down to dinner.

Workbook page 57

Reading and writing

Learners read the invitation from the story *Anansi and Turtle* and write their answers to the questions.

Answers

Anansi; Turtle; At the pond; 5 o'clock

Student's Book page 88

Reading, speaking and writing

This section involves reading and enjoying a rhyming poem with alliterative language. Read the poem with the learners and invite them to say what they notice about the poem. Discuss the meanings of any words that learners might be unsure of. Learners may like to add some words to their Word books.

Learners then work in pairs to read the poem before answering the questions in activity 2. Check that learners can read the questions and know what is expected of them.

Activity 3 asks the learners to find two words that rhyme, two nouns and two verbs.

Draw learners together to check answers, always referring to the text to clarify any errors.

Learners should work in groups of three to learn the poem. Each learner within the group learns one verse. They should then recite the poem in their groups to the class.

Answers

2 four characters; a mini mouse house

3 any two of the following – Myrtle, Merlin, Matty, Mummy MacMouse; mushrooms or marigolds. Pairs of rhyming words: mouse, house; too, stew; mice, nice; Nouns: meal, mouse, house, mushrooms, marigolds, moonlight, stew, mice. Proper nouns: Myrtle, Merlin, Matty, Mummy MacMouse. Verbs: make, mix, melt, says.

Weekly review

Use this rubric to assess learners' progress as they work through the activities this week. You can use the activities suggested beneath the table to follow up on your on-going assessment.

Level	Writing
■	With some support to keep to the theme of an event, can plan, write and decorate an invitation.
●	Can plan, write and decorate an invitation for an event with minimal support.
▲	Can confidently plan, write and decorate an invitation appropriately for an event.

Support: After discussion about the contents of an invitation reply, learners should plan and prepare a reply to an invitation.

Extension: Learners should plan, write and decorate a reply to an invitation.

Week 3

Key strands and substrands: Lesson outcomes

Reading

- Retell a story verbally
- Show understanding of characters in a story
- Know the letters of the alphabet in order
- Talk about texts, expressing preferences

Writing

- Plan writing by speaking
- Begin to write simple stories
- Use capital letters for proper nouns and at the start of sentences, and full stops
- Form upper-case letters correctly
- Record answers in lists

Speaking and listening

- Retell a story, enacting simple characters
- Take turns in speaking, listening to others and expressing own feelings and ideas
- Speak audibly and clearly with familiar people
- Show some non-verbal communication techniques
- Suggest how someone's non-verbal communication reflects their feelings

Resources

- Student's Book pages 82, 89–90
- Workbook pages 58–60
- PCM 40: End of unit task

Workbook page 58

Writing

If possible, have a selection of invitations to different events for the learners to look at. Discuss with the learners what invitations they and their families have received.

Are invitations always in the form of a card? Discuss what other ways someone might receive an invitation, for example by text, by email, by word of mouth. Elicit from learners what information should appear on an invitation – the person's name who sent invitation, the date of the event, the place of the event, the time of event, and so on. Discuss the importance of replying to an invitation.

Set out the format of the invitation as a model for learners to use.

Learners should decorate their invitation in a style that suits the type of invitation, for example to a wedding, to birthday party, to a bar mitzvah.

Student's Book page 89

Listening and speaking

Using the pictures, learners work in pairs to retell the story and act out the parts of Anansi and Turtle, while Anansi tries to get to the bottom of the pond for the food. Discuss with learners what they might say to each other and what kind of voices the characters might use. Encourage learners to add to the dialogue, making it as interesting as possible and to use expression. They should also think of their facial expressions and any gestures they might use. How would facial expression and gesture let the audience know how the character feels?

Draw learners together. Invite some learners to perform their dialogue and others to comment positively about the performances. For example, Anansi looked as if he was angry, I liked the way Turtle used his hands when he said, '…'

Speaking and writing

In pairs, learners then discuss a different ending for the story. What might have happened when Anansi went to visit Turtle? Bring learners together and invite them to say the new ending to the class. Learners then write new endings for the story. Ask learners to read their writing aloud to the class and invite others to say what they liked about the writing, giving examples: 'I liked the interesting words that you used', 'You used "and" to join words.'

Support: Some learners may need teacher support individually or as part of a small group to write a new ending.

Extension: Learners should work in groups of five, taking responsibility for one of the pictures on page 89, draw their own version of the picture and write a caption. You could display the pictures and captions.

Student's Book page 90

Speaking and listening

Learners should work in pairs. The first question is about Anansi's behaviour. The learners are asked to think about how Anansi behaved in the story. Give learners time to talk and share their ideas, monitoring that individuals are not dominating the conversations. Bring learners together to share their opinions.

The other questions are about Turtle's behaviour. How he behaved at the beginning of the story and how he behaved at the end of the story. Did his behaviour change? If so, was it a good change?

Bring the learners together to share their opinions and encourage them to explain why they think in a certain way about Turtle's behaviour.

Workbook page 59

Writing

1 In this activity, learners are asked to write the capital letter for the corresponding lower-case letter of the alphabet.

2 Learners write the names of characters from different units correctly, that is, using a capital letter at the beginning of each name.

Talk with learners about when capital letters are always used: at the beginning of sentences and names. Talk about other uses of capital letters – in headings, titles and for emphasis. For example:

- SPLASH! page 10 of The *Lonely Penguin*

Extension: Ask learners to write the title of the book (*The Big Red Bus*) in capital letters. They can decorate their title and colour the letters.

Answers

2 Rev, Shoo Rayner, Nut Hill, Dev, Joe's bakery, Bot

Thinking time

Ask learners to look through the book to remind themselves of the different units before discussing with learners which units they enjoyed most and why. Which type of books would they like to read more of?

- Do they enjoy fiction or non-fiction units?
- Do they enjoy stories or poetry?
- Do they enjoy fantasy stories or traditional stories?
- Do they enjoy stories about real life?

Workbook page 60

Support learners with this reflective task. Read the headings and explain how they should fill in the chart. Explain that they should self-assess how well they think they have completed the tasks in each unit. Reassure learners that there are no right or wrong answers.

Weekly review

Use this rubric to assess learners' progress as they work through the activities this week. You can use the activities suggested beneath the table to follow up on your on-going assessment.

Level	Reading	Listening and speaking
■	Can write a new ending for a story with some support.	Can speak in a group and answer questions. With support, can explain further when asked.
●	Can write a new ending for a story. Can use capital letters and full stops in more than one sentence.	Speaks well in a group. Can answer questions and develop answers with some support.
▲	Can write a new ending for a story. Can use capital letters and full stops in more than one sentence and spell familiar words accurately.	Speaks confidently in a group. Can answer questions, explaining further when asked.

Support: Learners should be given opportunities to work in small supportive groups to develop their confidence and ability to extend their answers.

Extension: Learners should be given the opportunity to develop their story writing to include a beginning, middle and end.

End of unit task

Use PCM 40 to assess how well learners are able to complete sentences and say what happened next in a story. Once learners have completed the work, ask them to share their answers with the class and let them assess their own work. Ask them to write a comment on their work at the end of the activity.

Phonics 1

Read the words. Write the word for each picture.

hat cat bat	 ________
bed red fed	 ________
tin fin pin	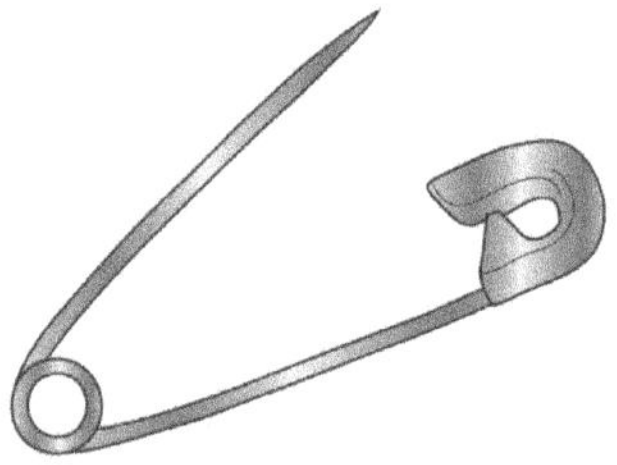 ________
but hut nut	 ________

Phonics 2

Read the words. Write the word for each picture.

bad bag bat

bet beg bed

hop top mop

wig dig fig

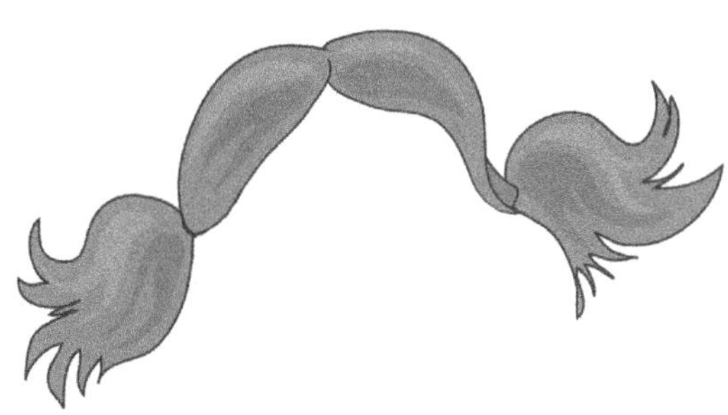

Phonics 3

Read the words. Write the word for each picture.

hut hat hit

pet pat pot

bid bed bud

fix fox fax

Phonics 4

Write the word for each picture.

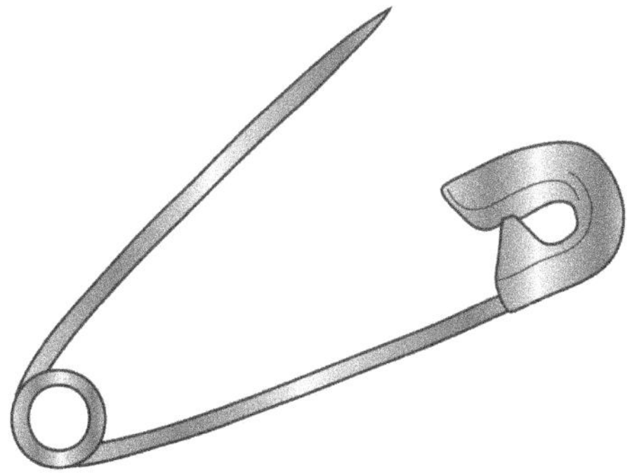

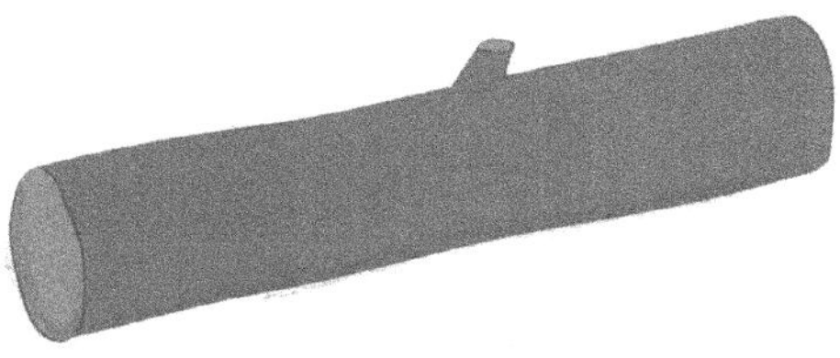

10

Phonics 5

Write the word for each picture.

6	
	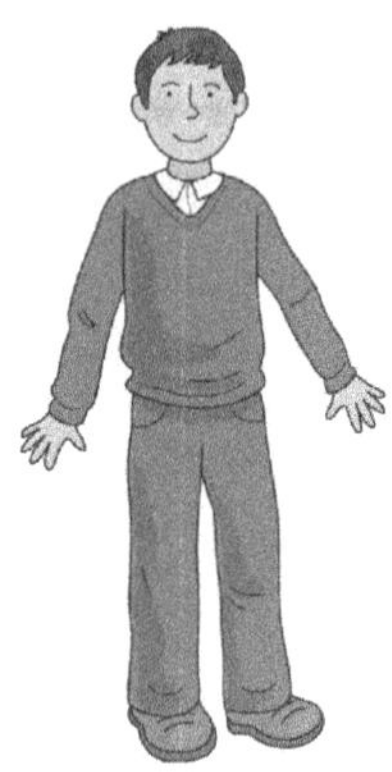

Phonics 6

Read the sentences.
Write the sentence that matches each picture.

	A man is in the van. A man is on the bus. ____________________
	The cat is on the bin. The cat is in the bin ____________________
	Gran can fix the tap. Gran can fix the tag. ____________________

Phonics 7

Write the words in the lists.

fat
sat

hat
____

____

lap
sap

____

____

man
ran

____

____

jag
wag

____

____

Phonics 8

Write the words in the lists.

top
pop

mop

den
men

fog
dog

met
wet

End of unit task

Read the instructions below.

1. **Cut along the dotted lines.**
2. **Put the sentences in order.**
3. **Read and check that the story makes sense.**
4. **Stick the sentences in order on to paper.**
5. **Read and check.**

We sit at the back of the bus.
I press the bell to get off.
We pass the pond and the clock.
We get on the bus.

Words ending in *–ing*

Write the sentences. Use words in the box.

cooking	jumping	kicking	lifting	reading

	He is ______________________
	He is ______________________
	They are ______________________
	He is ______________________
	They are ______________________

Phonics –*sh*

Complete the words. Write the words.

 fi______ ____________	 ______ell ____________
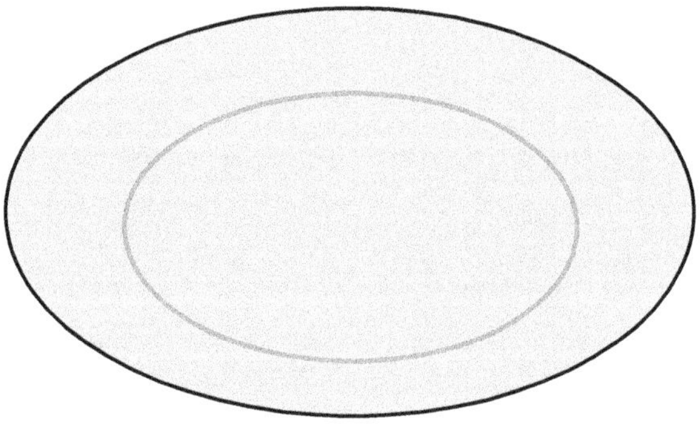 di______ ____________	 ______elf ____________

Phonics *sh*, *ch*, *th*, *wh*

Colour the pictures.

- *sh* words red
- *th* words blue
- *ch* words green
- *wh* words yellow

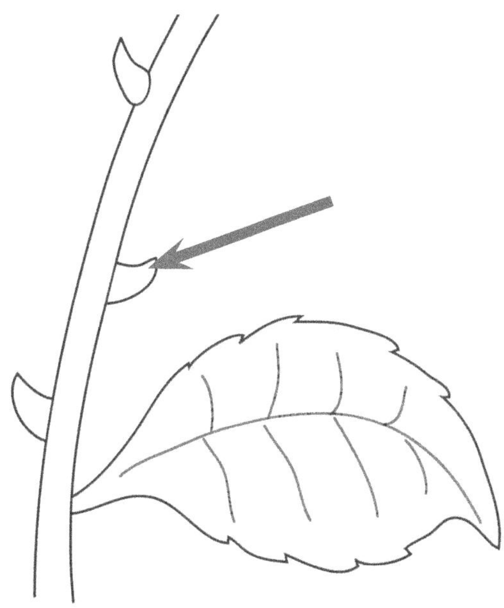

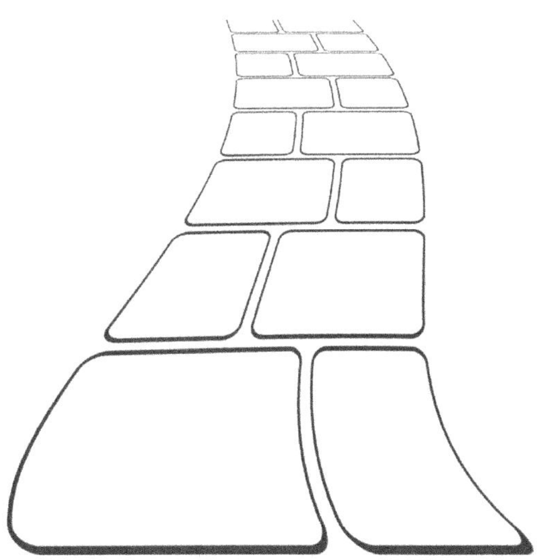

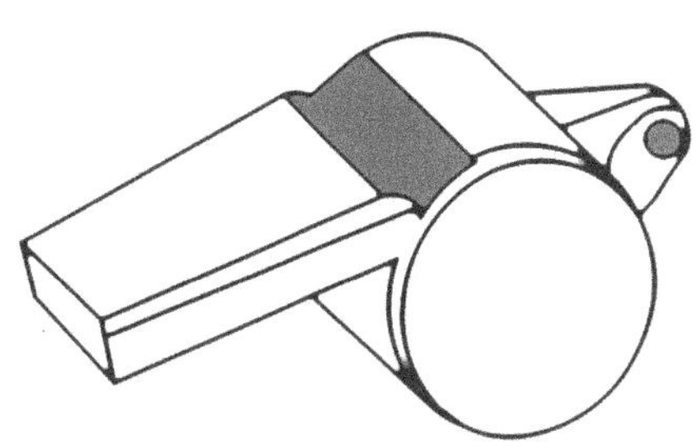

Phonics *sh, ch, th, wh*

Write the first two letters for each picture.

sh ch th wh

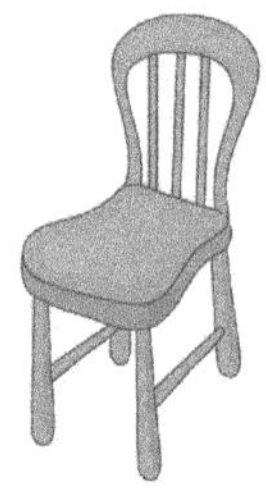

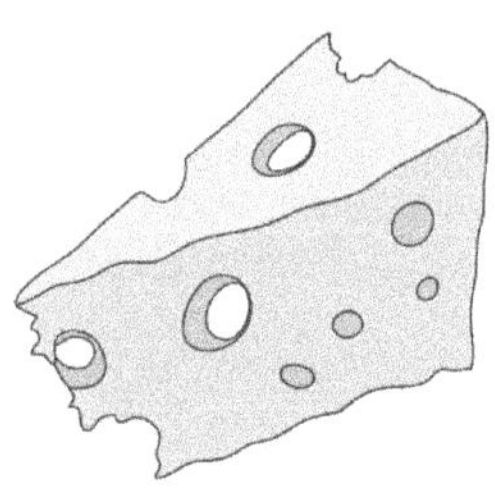

13

End of unit task

Read the instructions below.

1. **Cut along the dotted lines.**
2. **Put the sentences in order.**
3. **Read and check that the story makes sense.**
4. **Stick the sentences in order on to paper.**
5. **Read and check.**

Oops! I'm down with a thud!

I can jog with my frog.

I can jog in the mud.

And a fish on a dish.

Phonics *ng*

❶ Write the word for each picture.

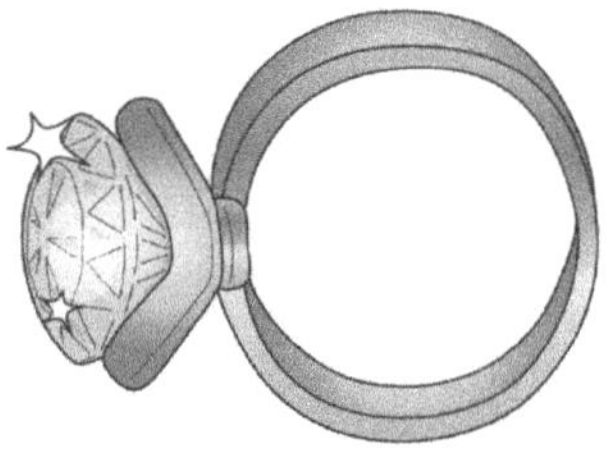

❷ Use the letters to make rhyming words.

s k	h r	l s
ring	bang	dong

Phonics *ck*

❶ Write the word for each picture.

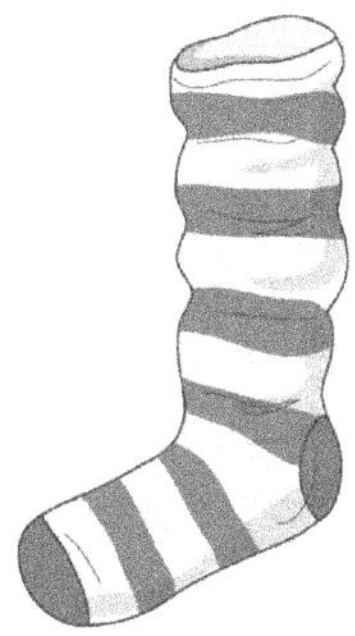

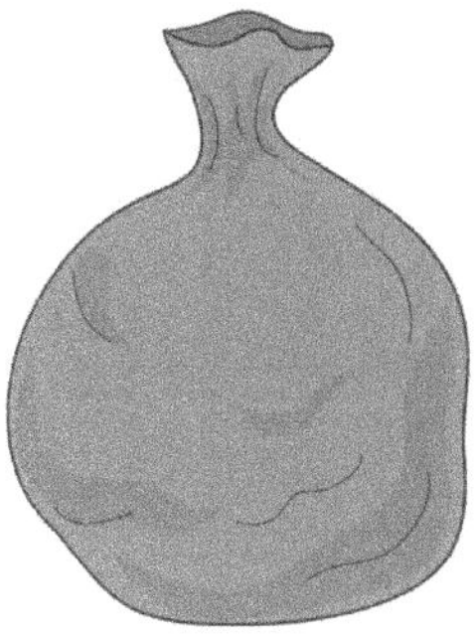

❷ Use the letters to make rhyming words.

k l	d s	d l
pick	lock	suck

Plurals

Read the words in the picture of the shop.

Write the words for two of each item.

add –*s*

____

____

add –*es*

____

____

End of unit task

Label the picture of the tiger. Use the words in the box.

paws	tail	stripes	nose	teeth	ears	eyes

Using 'and'

Bot got a card <u>and</u> a moon rock at the Moon Shop.

Write the phrases. Use 'and'.

a dog ______________ a ______________

a hat ______________ a ______________

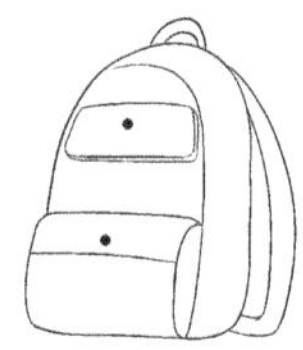

a fox ______________ a ______________

a bus ______________ a ______________

a bed ______________ a ______________

a cup ______________ a ______________

Phonics – adjacent consonants at the end of words

1 Circle the word ending. Write the word.

lf nd

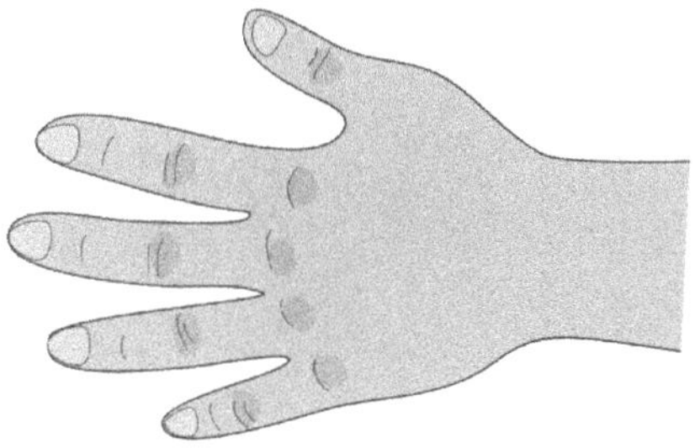

sk lk

mp ft

nd nk

2 Use the letters to make rhyming words.

j p	b s	m b
bump	land	send

Phonics – adjacent consonants at the beginning of words

1 Circle the word beginning. Write the word.

dr br 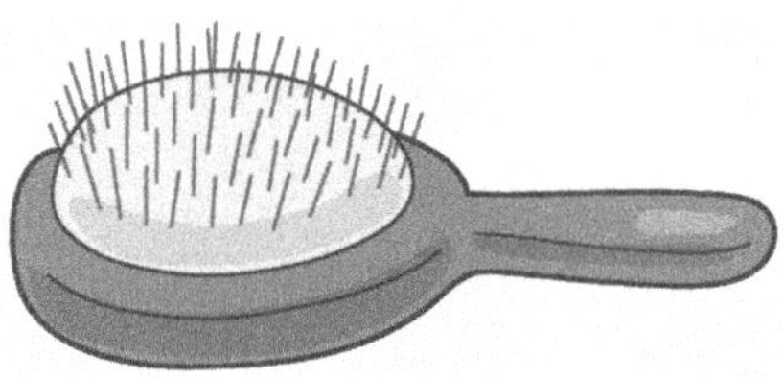	pr tr 
gr cr 	fr br 
dr br 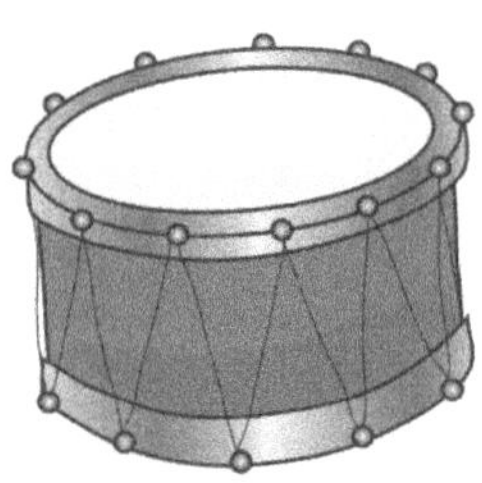	fr tr 

2 Complete the sentences.

- Dan plays the ______________________ in the band.
- The ______________________ hid in the grass.
- The ______________________ is on the rock.

Phonics – adjacent consonants at the beginning of words

1 Tick the word for each picture. Write the word.

swim ☐ swell ☐

skid ☐ skip ☐

swing ☐ swim ☐

stem ☐ step ☐

2 Complete the sentences.

- Zenib will stand on the top ______________________.
- Tim likes to ______________________ on the grass.
- Fran can ______________________ well.

Phonics – adjacent consonants at the beginning of words

Match the pictures with the words. Write the words.

trap ______________

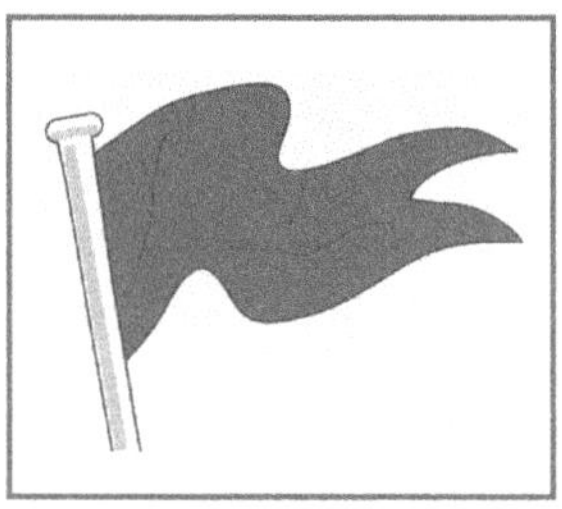

plug ______________

flag ______________

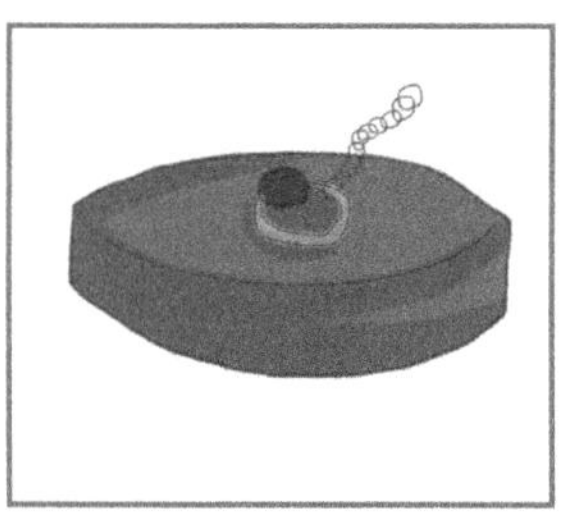

clock ______________

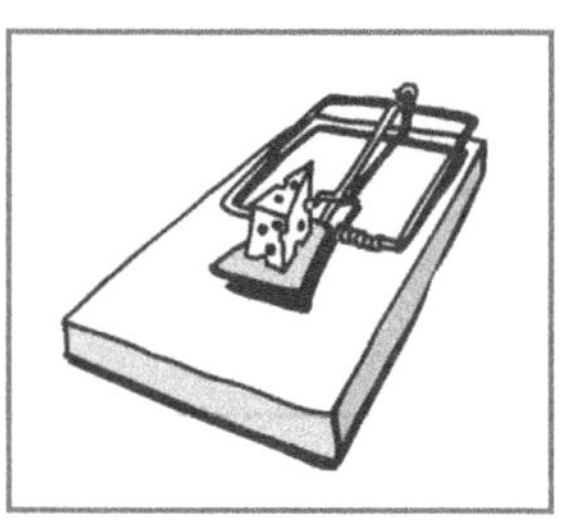

slug ______________

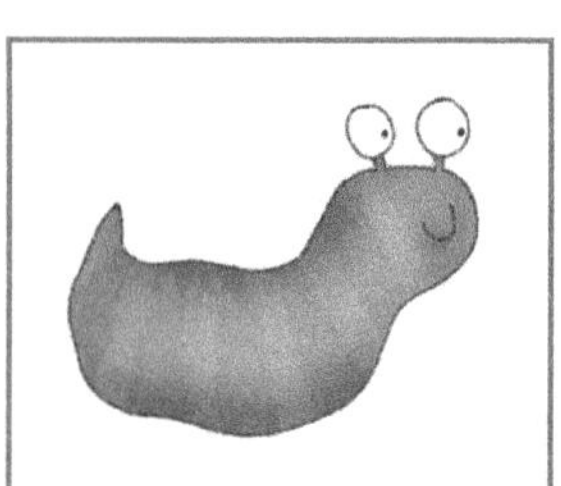

glasses ______________

Consonant-consonant-vowel-consonant words

Match the word to its meaning.

nest	a type of shoe
truck	a bird lays its eggs in it
clog	a small jumping animal
frog	a vehicle that carries things
flock	a sea animal that has a hard shell
crab	a musical instrument
drum	a collection of birds

End of unit task

Write the sentences.

	A ________________ on a ________________
	A ________________ on a ________________
	A ________________ on a ________________
	A ________________ on a ________________

Spelling common words

Complete the sentences. Use the words in the boxes.

Three funny ______________ were swimming in the sea.

fish fins

One funny fish said "______________ at me!"

Look Like

"I am ______________ and funny and red."

big bright

"I am the ______________ fish here," it said.

bright best

Then a ______________ fish came and swish, swish, swish...

big best

Write the next sentence in the story.

____

Phonics skills and context

Complete the story.

Three funny ________________ were swimming in the sea.

One funny fish said, "________________ at me!"

"I am bright ________________ funny ________________ red."

"I am the ________________ fish here," it said.

Then, a ________________ fish came and swish, swish, swish...

That was the ________________ of the funny red fish.

Two funny fish were swimming ________________ the sea.

One funny fish said, "Look at ________________!"

"I am yellow – as bright as the ________________!"

Write the next sentence in the story.

____

End of unit task

Read the poem. Write pairs of rhyming words.

Nut Tree

Small, brown, hard, round,
The nut is lying underground.

Now a shoot begins to show,
Now the shoot begins to grow.

Tall, taller, tall as can be,
The shoot is growing into a tree.

And branches grow and stretch and spread
With twigs and leaves above your head.

And on a windy day
The nut tree bends, the branches sway.

The leaves fly off and whirl around,
And nuts go tumbling to the ground.
Small, brown, hard and round.

by Julia Donaldson

______________ ______________

______________ ______________

______________ ______________

______________ ______________

a or *an*?

1 Label the fruits. Use *a* or *an*.

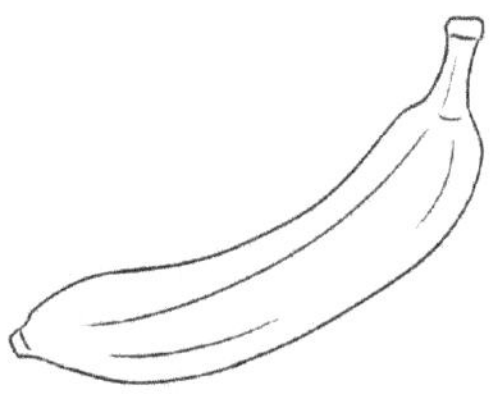 ____a____ banana	 __________ peach
 __________ apple	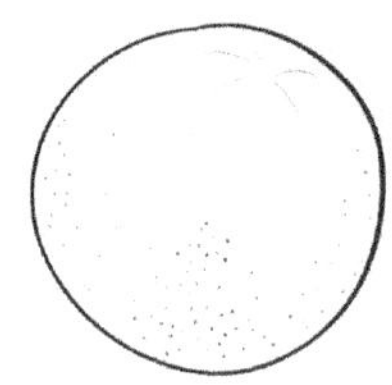 __________ orange
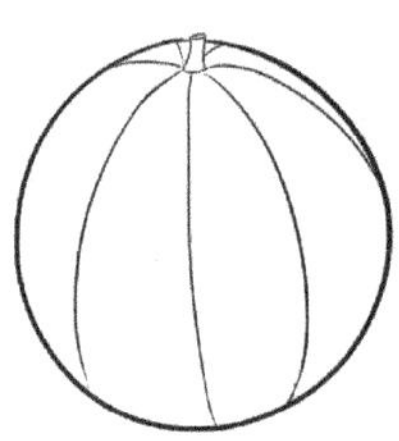 __________ melon	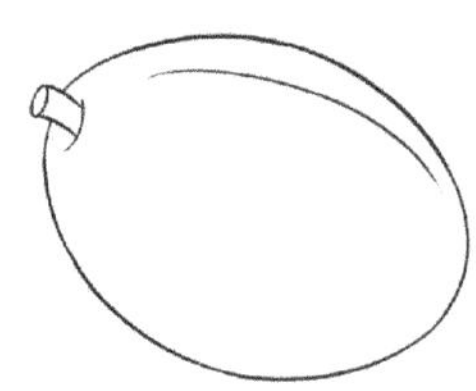 __________ plum
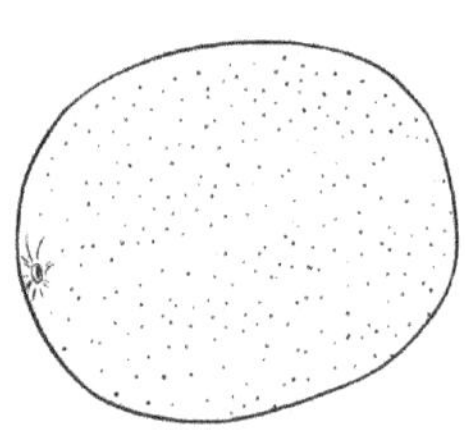 __________ kiwi	 __________ pineapple

2 Choose one fruit and write a sentence about it.

____

____

End of unit task

Match the foods with their food group.

Fruit and vegetables

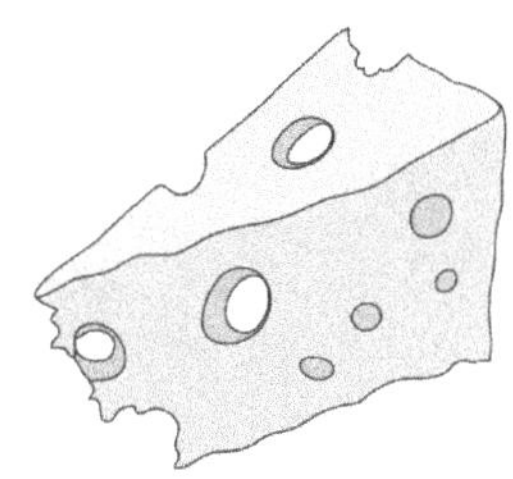

Bread and cereal

Fish and seafood

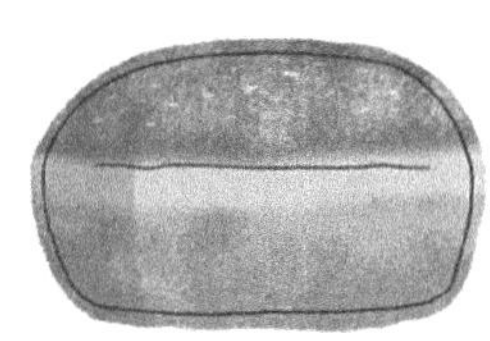

Dairy and eggs

Phonics *ee*

❶ Write the word for each picture.

		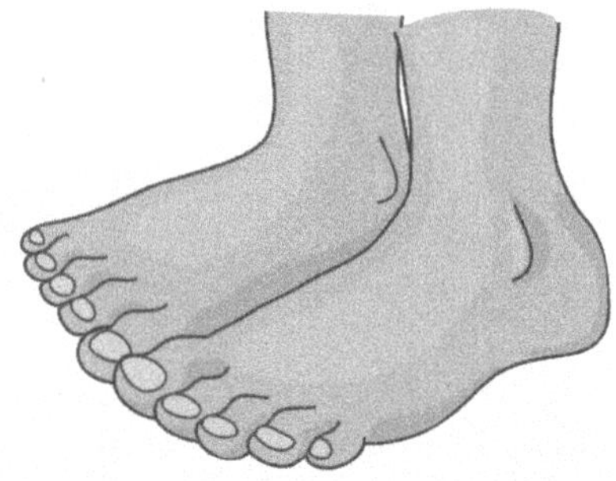
		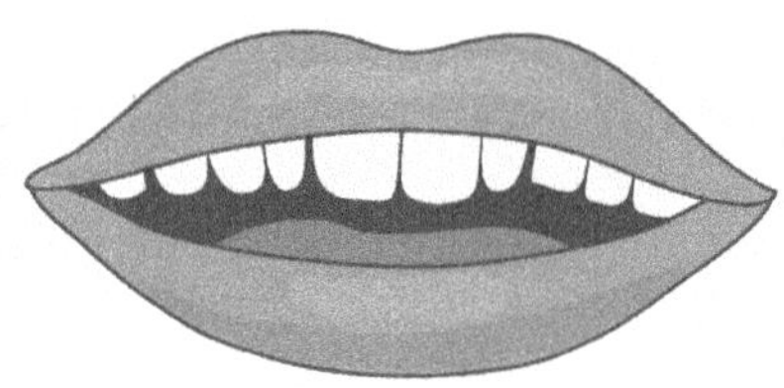

❷ Complete the sentences.

- The ______________________________ are lost on the hill.
- The ______________________________ stung my leg.
- The nest is in the ______________________________.
- I brush my ______________________________ at night.

Phonics *oa*

1 Write the word to name each picture.

		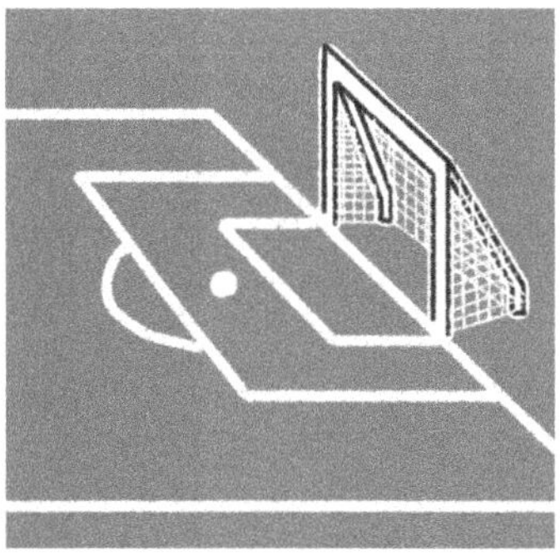
______	______	______

2 Use the letters to make rhyming words.

fl thr	t r
goat	coast
______	______
______	______

3 Complete the sentences.

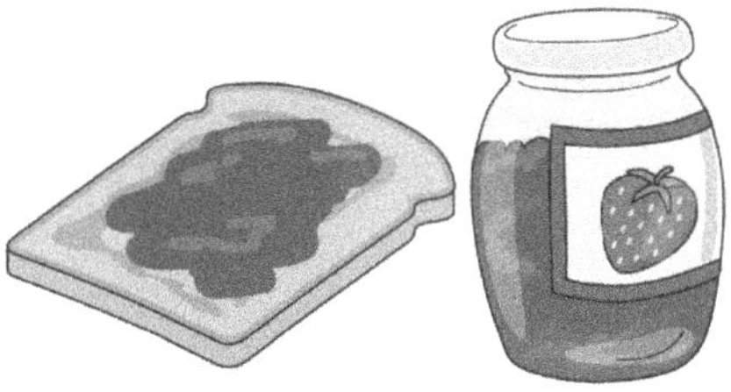

- Joan had ______ and jam.

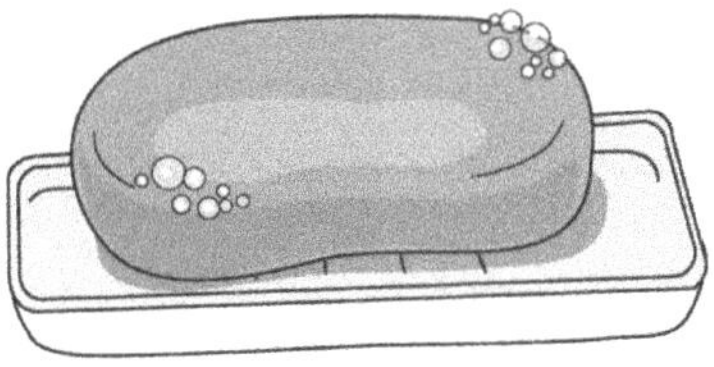

- The ______ fell in the sink.

- Krisha has a hood on her ______.

Phonics *ai*

1 Write the word to name each picture.

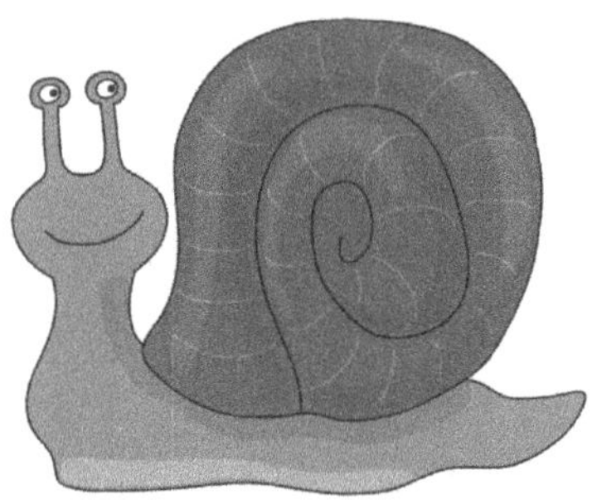

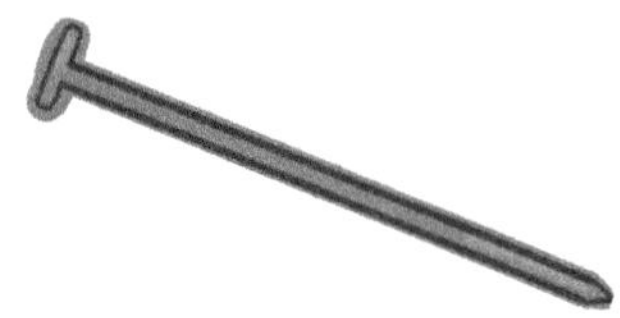

2 Write the three words that rhyme in question 1.

3 Write words that rhyme with 'pail'.
Use the letters in the box.

f j r s t

Words with long vowels

1 Find a word for each clue. Match the clue to the word.

we wash with it	wheel
a car has four of them	Spain
a cat has one	soap
the name of a country	three
a young horse	tail
the number after two	foal

2 Write a clue for each word.

road ______________________________

feet ______________________________

brain ______________________________

End of unit task

Write a sentence to tell what happened in each picture.

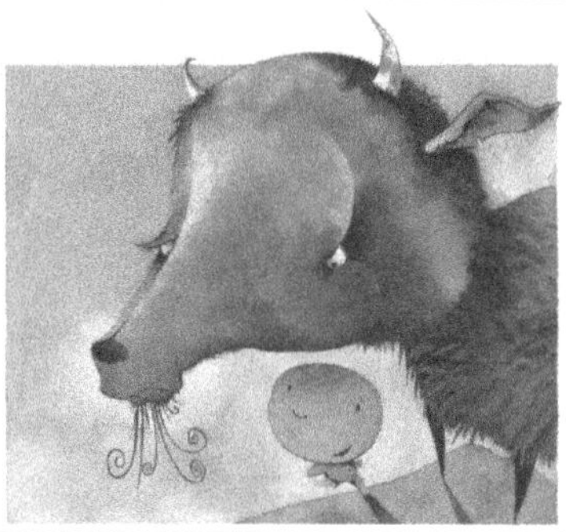	

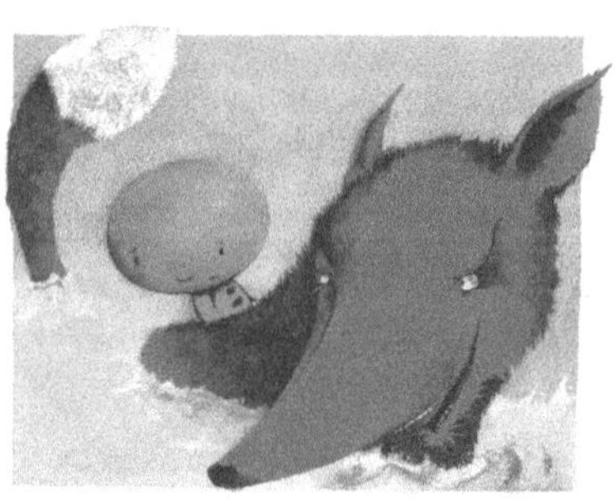	

Words ending in –*ed* and –*ing*

Complete the table. Use the endings –*ed* and –*ing*.

lick	licked	licking
grunt		
melt		
land		
dust		
print		
rest		
shift		

Words ending in *–ed* and *–ing*

1 Add *–ed* or *–ing* to the words. Write the words.

The girl walk___ to school yesterday. ______________

Anna is play___ with the ball. ______________

The children are jump___ with ropes. ______________

The ice cream melt___ in the sun. ______________

We print___ the letters at school. ______________

Preet is bend___ down to pick up the book.

____

2 Write sentences. Use the words in the box.

walking	jumping

____

____

Phonics *oo*

1 Write the word to name each picture.

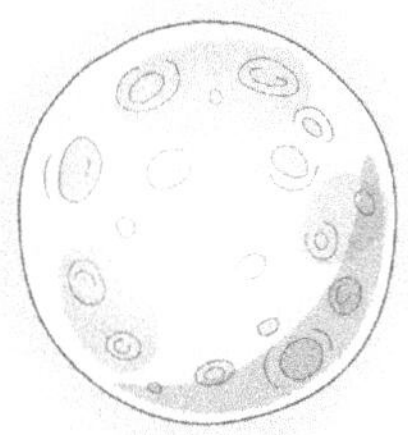

2 Complete the sentences. Use the words from question 1.

- The cat is on the ______.
- The ______ is in the pot.
- Josh sat on the ______.

3 Use the letters to make rhyming words.

m s	r sh	gr br
noon	boot	room
______	______	______
______	______	______

End of unit task

Write the word to name each picture.

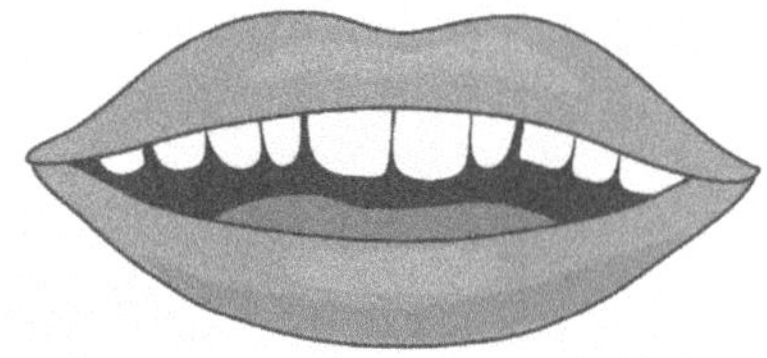

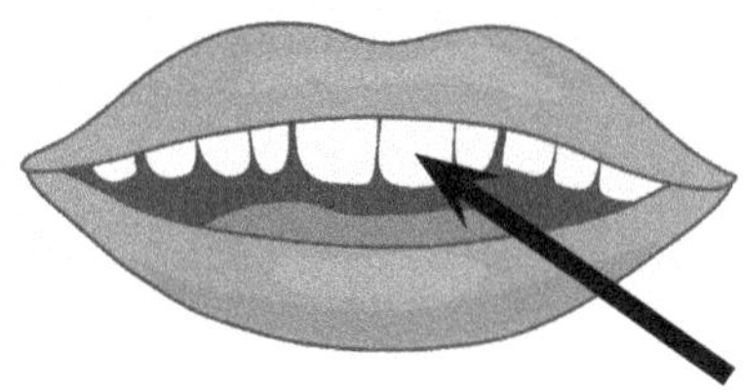

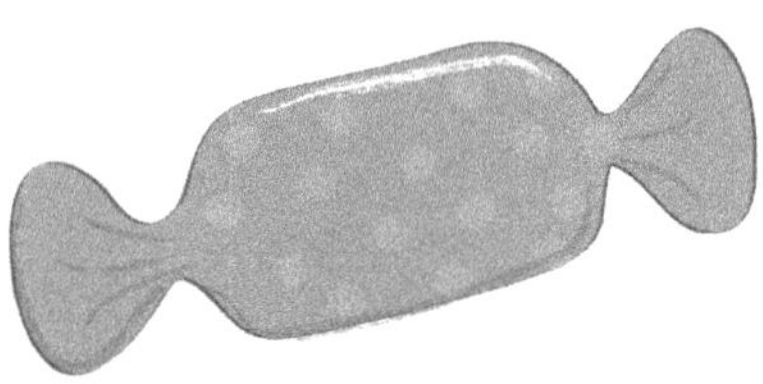

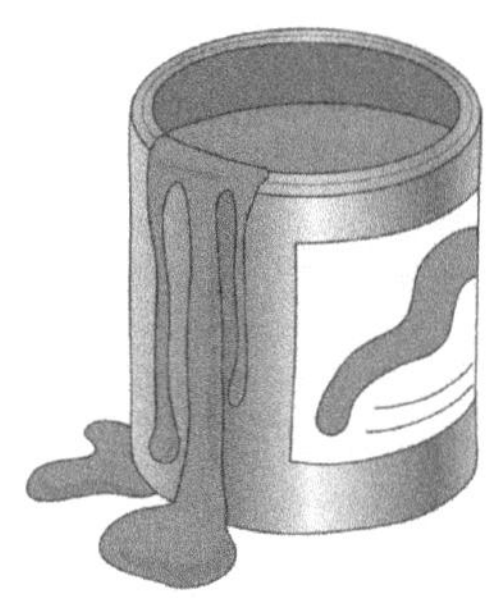

End of unit task

❶ Complete the sentences.

When Turtle returned ______ saw that ________ plates were empty.

"Why did you not ________ for ________?" asked Turtle.

"You were too ________ and I ________ hungry," answered Anansi.

❷ Write what happened next.

Cambridge Global Perspectives™

Below are some examples of lessons in *Collins International Primary English Stage 1* which could be used to develop the Global Perspectives skills. The notes in italics suggest how the English activity can be made more relevant to Global Perspectives.

Please note that the examples below link specifically to the learning objectives in the Global Perspectives curriculum framework for Stage 1. However, skills development in a wider sense is embedded throughout this course and teachers are encouraged to promote research, analysis, evaluation, reflection, collaboration and communication as general best practice.

Cambridge Global Perspectives skills	Learning Objectives for Stage 1	Collins International Primary English Stage 1
RESEARCH	Conducting research • Begin to participate in simple investigations and ask basic questions to find information and opinions	• Unit 1, Week 3, Reading 3–4: SB p10, TG p28 *Learners are introduced to library research as they look for books of different genres.* • Unit 3, Week 2, Reading and writing 2–4: SB p27, TG p44 *Learners are introduced to basic research and find some simple information.*
	Recording findings • Record information on a given topic in pictograms or simple graphic organisers	• Unit 1, Week 1, Listening and speaking Extension: TG p20 *Give learners support to collect and record the information in a simple tally chart. Then guide them to record this information in a pictograph.* • Unit 6, Week 2, Reading and writing Extension: TG pp72–73 *Use this activity to introduce the use of pictograms.*
ANALYSIS	Identifying perspectives • Say something known about a topic	• Unit 2, Week 2, Speaking and writing (incl. Extension): SB p17, TG p34 *After learners have completed the pair work and drawn a picture, ask them to do a show and tell using the picture.*
	Interpreting data • Talk about information recorded in pictograms or graphical organisers	• Unit 6, Week 1, Listening and speaking: SB p51, TG p69 *Ask learners the questions in the TG, and other similar questions, to focus on how the poster represents information about amounts.*
EVALUATION	Evaluating arguments • State an opinion about a given topic	*The Thinking time sections at the end of many units give opportunities for learners to give their opinions on given topics. For example:* • Unit 2, Week 3, Thinking time: SB p20, TG p39 • Unit 3, Week 3, Thinking time: SB p30, TG p48 • Unit 5, Week 3, Thinking time: SB p50, TG p66 • Unit 6, Week 3, Thinking time: SB p60, TG p77 • Unit 8, Week 3, Thinking time: SB p80, TG p94
REFLECTION	Personal viewpoints • Talk about what has been learned during an activity with support	• Unit 2, Week 3, Listening and speaking: SB p20, TG p39 *Give learners time and support as they express answers to these questions in the final plenary session.*
	Personal learning • Talk about something liked in a particular activity	*The Thinking time sections at the end of some units give opportunities for learners to express what they enjoyed in an activity or unit. For example:* • Unit 1, Week 3, Thinking time: SB p10, TG p29 • Unit 4, Week 3, Thinking time: SB p40, TG p57 • Unit 9, Week 3, Thinking time: SB p90, TG p102
COLLABORATION	Engaging in teamwork • Work positively with others	• Unit 1, Week 3, Role play: SB p8, TG p28 *Focus on the need for learners to listen to each other and interact appropriately to be able to do the role play successfully.* • Unit 7, Week 3, Reading and writing Extension: TG p85 *Give groups time to discuss and prepare their performances. Monitor as they work and guide them to listen to each other and collaborate.* • Unit 9, Week 3, Listening and speaking: SB p89, TG p101 *Give pairs plenty of time to discuss and prepare their dialogues and performances. Monitor as they work and guide them to listen to each other and collaborate.*
COMMUNICATION	Communicating information • Answer questions with relevant information about a given topic	*There are a number of simple information exchange activities included. For example:* • Unit 1, Week 1, Listening and speaking: SB p1, TG p20 *The Extension activity also gives the opportunity to introduce conducting research and recording findings.* • Unit 2, Week 1, Listening and speaking: SB p11, TG p30 • Unit 6, Week 3, Listening and speaking (both activities): SB p 59, TG p76

